NORTHERN CALIFORNIA
DOG
OWNERS
GUIDE

THE STARTER BOOK

BOB AND LAURA CHRISTIANSEN
CANINE LEARNING CENTER
CARLSBAD, CALIFORNIA

Printed in the United States of America

Published by

Canine Learning Center

Post Office Box 2010
Carlsbad, California 92018
619 931-1820

Library of Congress Catalog Card No. 94-69455
ISBN 1-884421-21-0
Typesetting and design by **Word Wizards**®, Oceanside, California
Cover design and graphics by **Patton Brothers**®, San Diego, California

DISCLAIMER

Every precaution has been taken to avoid errors, mistakes and omissions. No liability is accepted for any errors, mistakes or omissions which may occur, no matter how caused.

CAUTION

Dog Owners Guide is unable to assume any responsibility or liability for any listing. Inclusion in this publication does not constitute an endorsement, recommendation or guarantee by the authors or the publisher for any product, organization, or person. This publication is for general instructive use only. Readers are advised to make their own inquiries and to seek out conscientious service providers who subscribe to high standards. *Dog Owners Guide* reserves the right to refuse publication to anyone not acting in the best interests of dogs.

Books are available at special discounts for bulk purchases to dog-related charitable activities, educational groups, breed clubs or breeders.

TO THE READER

This book is intended to be a helpful all-inclusive local resource guide for dog lovers in Northern California. Every major facet of dog ownership is covered and at your fingertips. In writing this book, we have attempted to put forth useful, accurate information that is readily accessible to all owners, especially those who are contemplating acquiring a dog or who have recently purchased a puppy and are inexperienced in what to expect. Most dog owners have the best intentions when they obtain a cute little puppy, however, frustrations can soon develop and frustration can soon lead to anger, neglect and abandonment. Don't let that happen to you! We sincerely hope and believe the information in this book will help ease your access to dog-related organizations, help you understand dog behavior and help you achieve a successful relationship with your dog.

We would like to thank all those animal lovers who have helped contribute to this book: Ann Wilde, Mary Wamsley, Claire Newick, Helen Hamilton, Diane Calkins, Captain Theresa Williams of the San Diego Animal Control, Ellyn Sisser, Laure Krisch from the Peninsula Humane Society, the San Francisco Humane Society, Nancy Lyon,Ohlone Human Society, and special thanks to Flo Bell for all her hard work, Dr. Robert Cartin DVM, Mission Animal Hospital, Helen Woodward Animal Center, and all the breeders and breed clubs. Special thanks to All Creatures Hospital, Dr. Michael Mulvany DVM and Jean Hamilton for their input.

We would like to hear what you think. If you have any ways of improving this publication, please write to:

Canine Learning Center
P.O. Box 2010
Carlsbad, CA 92018

Contents

Ten Things A Dog Asks Of Its Family

1. My life is likely to last 10 to 15 years. Any permanent separation from you will be painful for me. Remember that before you buy me.

2. Do not break my spirit with harsh treatment. Your patience and understanding will more quickly teach me the things you would have me learn.

3. Place your trust in me, it's crucial for my well-being.

4. Don't be angry with me for long, and don't lock me up as a punishment. You have your work, your entertainment, and your friends, I have only you and I like being with you.

5. Talk to me. Even if I don't understand your words I understand the tone of your voice when you are speaking to me, especially when you use friendly tones.

6. Be aware that I am normally a social animal; however, I need to make positive associations at a young age to feel confident and well-adjusted around other dogs and humans.

7. Remember that I was bred for activity, both mental and physical, and I enjoy playing games, taking walks and an occasional good run.

8. Before you scold me for being uncooperative, obstinate, or lazy, ask yourself if something may be bothering me. Perhaps I'm not getting the right food. I may need medical attention, or I may just be getting old. But keep in mind I respond very well to praise.

9. Take care of me when I get old; you, too, will grow old.

10. Remember that I only want to love and please you so treat me kindly. No heart is more grateful.

1

Should You Get A Dog?

Things to Consider Before Deciding on a New Dog

1. What breed will you choose? Purebred or mixed breed? Each breed was bred for certain functions and all have different exercise, training, and grooming requirements. Mixed breeds make wonderful pets. The trick is to find the right size, weight, coat and *temperament* to fit your family. Purebred dogs are genetically more predictable.

2. Who will be the one to walk, feed, clean up after, train, play with and groom the dog, get him licensed and provide medical care? Be realistic, it's a job for adults or responsible older children. If you have children, can you teach them to be respectful of the new puppy?

3. Have you considered the costs involved in caring for a dog, like food, equipment, vet bills, a license and insurance? (Min. $300.)

4. Do you have permission from your landlord, preferably in writing?

5. How will you teach him the rules of the house? Chewing, barking, digging, housesoiling, etc., are normal dog behaviors. Dogs usually continue these behaviors until effectively trained. Can your family accept this and be patient, kind and consistent during the teaching process?

6. Do you have enough space to house the dog properly? How will you keep the dog under control? Barking and free-roaming pets are a nuisance to neighbors, endanger the dog, and against the law.

7. Will you mind hair shedding, fleas and odors (varies from dog to dog), or will it annoy and burden you? Do you, your friends or relatives have an allergic reaction to pet hair?

8. Will you be a responsible pet owner by providing vaccinations and spaying or neutering your pet?

9. Do you have enough time and energy for daily activities? Will it be difficult to spend the time to train, exercise and groom? Will the pet blend into your routine or will it become an annoyance or burden?

10. Do you have the emotional stability and staying power to be a responsible owner for the lifetime of your dog?

Dog Facts

There are 52.3 million dogs that live in the US, 37.9% of all households own dogs, 1.5 dogs average per household.

Each year 8.4 million dogs are euthanized, that means one every 3.7 seconds.

Of the estimated 52.3 million dogs, a little less than 27% end-up in shelters.

Of the 13.9 million, 44% or 6.1 million are surrendered by owners.

Over 56% or 7.8 million are picked-up as strays.

Approximately 60% of all dogs entering a shelter are euthanized, 15% reclaimed, 25% adopted.

One out of five dogs born finds a permanent home.

Twenty-five to forty percent of shelter dogs are purebred.

There are approximately 5.7 million dogs in the state of California (35.7% of all households).

Reasons for Surrender

1. Landlord objects to complaints from other tenants — behavior problems
2. Not enough time for the dog
3. Owner moves

What You Can Do to Solve Pet Overpopulation

1. Spay/Neuter your pet at an early age and encourage others to do the same.
2. Don't be an uneducated owner. Take a basic obedience dog class and learn fundamental dog behavior.

3. Safeguard your pets. Don't let your dog roam, especially if your pet is unaltered. Properly secure unspayed bitches (especially while they are in season) from unplanned matings. Most accidental litters are a result of roamers who meet up with bitches who are in season.

4. Make sure identification is in place and secured with an O ring. Dog licenses are the main way lost dogs get found.

5. Acquire your pet from a reputable local breeder or animal shelter.

6. Leave breeding to knowledgeable, experienced professional breeders who are dedicated to improving the standards of the breed.

7. Make a donation to a low-cost spay/neuter non-profit organization like Pet Assistance.

8. Take responsibility for your pet. If, for whatever reason, you need to give up your dog, make every effort to find a good home. Don't kid yourself into thinking someone will come to the shelter and give your dog a home on their farm. Statistics tell us that approximately 60% of all dogs that enter shelters will be euthanized.

9. If you are experiencing behavior problems, get the help of a trained professional. Call your veterinarian or pet store and ask for a referral to a good behaviorist or trainer. Many dog problems are unknowingly caused by minor owner handling errors.

10. If you are going to move, take the pet with you. Talk to your future landlord and explain that you have a well-behaved dog. Take an AKC Good Citizenship Test and show the certificate to your landlord. Offer to make a dog security deposit that will protect the owner from financial loss to his or her property.

11. If you never have bred before and you have the slightest inclination to breed your dog,

don't. Too many stray and unwanted dogs are the product of casual breedings or accidental breedings. When a dog is born from an unplanned litter, chances are it will be condemned to a life of misery, deprivation and death.

Note regarding early-age spaying/neutering: The following organizations endorse early-age (8-16 weeks) spay/neutering to stem the overpopulation of dogs and cats: the Humane Society of the United States (HSUS), the American Kennel Club (AKC) and the American Humane Association (AHA). The American Veterinary Medical Association (AVMA) supports the concept of early-age ovariohysterectomies/gonadectomies in dogs and cats.

Don't be part of the problem —
Be part of the solution!

2

The Breeds

AKC Popularity Ranking 1993

Rank	Breed	Size	Lbs.	Coat
1	Labrador Retriever	Large	55-75	Short
2	Rottweiler	Very Large	80-135	Short
3	German Shepherd Dog	Large	65-85	Medium
4	Cocker Spaniel	Small	25-28	Medium
5	Golden Retriever	Large	60-75	Medium
6	Poodle (Toy)	Miniature	8-10	Medium
6	Poodle (Standard)	Large	45-65	Medium
6	Poodle (Miniature)	Miniature	15-17	Medium
7	Beagle	Small	15-20	Short
8	Dachshund (Short-haired)	Small	16-22	Short
8	Dachshund (Long-haired)	Small	16-22	Medium
8	Dachshund (Wire-haired)	Small	16-22	Short
9	Dalmatian	Large	45-65	Short
10	Shetland Sheepdog	Miniature	16-18	Medium
11	Pomeranian	Miniature	3-7	Medium
12	Yorkshire Terrier	Miniature	5-7	Long
13	Shih Tzu	Miniature	12-15	Long
14	Miniature Schnauzer	Miniature	14-17	Short
15	Chow Chow	Large	60-70	Medium
16	Chihuahua (Long)	Miniature	5-6	Medium
16	Chihuahua (Smooth)	Miniature	5-6	Short
17	Boxer	Large	65-70	Short
18	Siberian Husky	Large	35-60	Medium
19	Doberman Pinscher	Large	60-75	Short
20	English Springer Spaniel	Medium	44-55	Medium
21	Basset Hound	Medium	40-60	Short
22	Chinese Shar-Pei	Medium	40-55	Short
23	Maltese	Miniature	4-6	Long
24	Lhasa Apso	Miniature	13-16	Long

Dog Owners Guide

Rank	Breed	Size	Lbs.	Coat
25	Boston Terrier	Small	13-25	Short
26	Pekingese	Miniature	12-14	Long
27	Collie (Rough)	Large	50-75	Long
27	Collie (Smooth)	Large	50-75	Short
28	Pug	Miniature	14-18	Short
29	Miniature Pinscher	Miniature	8-9	Short
30	German Shorthaired Pointer	Large	45-70	Short
31	Brittany	Medium	30-40	Medium
32	Bichon Frise	Small	11-15	Medium
33	Bulldog	Medium	40-50	Short
34	Akita (Japanese)	Very Large	75-100	Medium
35	Great Dane	Giant	120-150	Short
36	W. Highland White Terrier	Miniature	15-18	Medium
37	Scottish Terrier	Small	18-22	Medium
38	Corgi, Pembroke Welsh	Small	26-30	Short
39	Samoyed	Large	40-75	Medium
40	St. Bernard	Giant	145-165	Medium
41	Weimaraner	Large	55-85	Short
42	Alaskan Malamute	Large	75-85	Medium
43	Cairn Terrier	Miniature	13-14	Medium
44	Australian Shepherd	Large	45-65	Medium
45	Chesapeake Bay Retriever	Large	55-75	Short
46	Keeshond	Medium	35-40	Medium
47	Great Pyrenees Mountain Dog	Giant	90-115	Medium
48	Airedale Terrier	Medium	45-60	Short
49	Mastiff	Giant	170-180	Short
50	Schipperke	Miniature	15-17	Short
51	Old English Sheepdog	Very Large	90-100	Long
52	Newfoundland	Giant	120-150	Medium
53	Irish Setter	Large	60-70	Medium
54	Fox Terrier (Wire)	Small	16-18	Short
55	Norwegian Elkhound	Medium	45-55	Medium
56	Papillon	Miniature	7-8	Medium
57	Silky Terrier	Miniature	8-10	Long
58	Vizsla (Hungarian)	Medium	50-60	Short
59	Bullmastiff	Giant	100-130	Short
60	Italian Greyhound	Miniature	6-8	Short
61	Rhodesian Ridgeback	Large	65-75	Short
62	Bouvier des Flandres	Very Large	90-100	Medium
63	Whippet	Small	23-25	Short
64	Australian Cattle Dog	Medium	35-50	Short
65	American Eskimo Dogs (Std)	Small	25-35	Medium
66	Basenji	Small	22-24	Short

Rank	Breed	Size	Lbs.	Coat
67	Bloodhound	Very Large	80-110	Short
68	Soft Coated Wheaten Terrier	Medium	35-40	Long
69	Afghan Hound	Large	50-70	Long
70	German Wirehaired Pointer	Large	50-75	Medium
71	Bernese Mountain Dog	Very Large	75-105	Medium
72	Gordon Setter	Large	40-80	Medium
73	English Cocker Spaniel	Small	26-34	Medium
74	Borzoi	Very Large	60-105	Medium
75	Bull Terrier	Medium	40-59	Short
76	Irish Wolfhound	Giant	105-120	Medium
77	Giant Schnauzer	Large	75-95	Medium
78	Am. Staffordshire Terrier	Medium	40-70	Short
79	Japanese Chin	Miniature	4-9	Medium
80	Fox Terrier (Smooth)	Small	16-18	Short
81	Shiba Inu	Small	15-28	Medium
82	Chinese Crested	Miniature	10	Hairless
83	French Bulldog	Small	19-28	Short
84	English Setter	Large	50-70	Medium
85	Portuguese Water Dog	Medium	40-59	Medium
86	Welsh Terrier	Miniature	19-20	Short
87	Bearded Collie	Medium	40-59	Long
88	Corgi, Cardigan Welsh	Small	28-33	Short
89	Border Terrier	Small	11-15	Medium
90	Tibetan Terrier	Small	22-30	Long
91	Belgian Sheepdog	Large	60-89	Medium
92	Pointers	Large	50-75	Short
93	Brussels Griffon	Miniature	8-10	Medium
94	Standard Schnauzer	Medium	30-50	Medium
95	Kerry Blue Terrier	Medium	30-40	Short
96	Saluki	Large	55-65	Short
97	Belgian Tervuren	Large	60-75	Medium
98	Manchester Terrier, Toy	Miniature	7-12	Short
98	Manchester Terrier, Standard	Small	13-22	Short
99	Australian Terrier	Miniature	12-14	Medium
100	Belgian Malinois	Large	60-89	Short
101	Flat-Coated Retriever	Large	60-70	Long
102	Kuvaszok	Very Large	80-115	Medium
103	Tibetan Spaniel	Miniature	9-15	Medium
104	Staffordshire Bull Terrier	Medium	28-38	Short
105	Norwich Terrier	Miniature	11-12	Short
106	Briard	Large	60-89	Long
107	American Water Spaniel	Small	25-45	Medium
108	Welsh Springer Spaniel	Medium	35-40	Medium

Dog Owners Guide

Rank	Breed	Size	Lbs.	Coat
109	Norfolk Terrier	Miniature	11-12	Short
110	Irish Terrier	Small	25-27	Short
111	Lakeland Terrier	Miniature	10-17	Short
112	Komondor (Hungarian)	Very Large	80-95	Long
113	Pulik (Hungarian)	Small	26-39	Long
114	Scottish Deerhound	Very Large	75-110	Short
115	Bedlington Terrier	Small	17-23	Medium
116	Affenpinscher	Miniature	7-8	Medium
117	Petits Bassets Griffons Vendee	Small	35-45	Medium
118	English Toy Spaniel	Miniature	9-12	Medium
119	Wirehaired Pointing Griffon	Medium	50-60	Medium
119	Black and Tan Coonhound	Large	65-90	Short
121	Finnish Spitz	Small	24-35	Medium
122	Greyhound	Large	60-70	Short
123	Clumber Spaniel	Medium	35-60	Medium
124	Irish Water Spaniel	Large	45-65	Medium
125	Curley-Coated Retriever	Large	60-65	Medium
126	Pharoah Hound	Medium	40-60	Short
127	Miniature Bull Terrier	Small	23-28	Short
128	Skye Terrier	Small	27-28	Long
129	Dandie Dinmont Terrier	Small	18-24	Medium
130	Field Spaniel	Medium	35-50	Medium
131	Ibizan Hound	Medium	42-50	Short
132	Sealyham Terrier	Small	23-24	Medium
132	Otterhound	Very Large	65-115	Long
134	Sussex Spaniel	Medium	35-45	Medium
135	Harrier	Medium	40-59	Short
136	American Foxhound	Large	60-70	Short
137	English Foxhound	Large	70-75	Short
Misc	Jack Russell Terrier	Miniature	12-15	Short
Misc	Border Collies	Medium	35-50	Medium
Misc	Cavalier King Charles Spnl.	Miniature	13-18	Long
Misc	Spinoni Italiano	Large	50-60	Short
Misc	Greater Swiss Mt. Dog	Very Large	120-130	Short
Misc	Canaan Dog	Medium	35-55	Short

Breed Groups

Sporting Breeds— This group consists of the gun dogs used in the field with the hunter. They hunt principally by picking up scents carried in the air. They are separated mainly into three divisions depending upon the purpose for which they were developed. These are:

Pointers and Setters are breeds that locate game far ahead of the hunter. These breeds will indicate the position of the game by assuming a peculiarly rigid stance or by pointing their nose toward the scent of the game.

Retrievers were bred for duty in the field. They are experts in "finding and returning" game to the hunter. They are powerful swimmers.

Spaniels were developed to work in rough cover and close to the gun when locating, flushing and retrieving game.

The Hounds— This group consists of the breeds which hunt animals and run down game with their athleticism and speed. Some trail by *scent* like the Bloodhound. Others chase by *sight* like the Greyhound and Afghan, while still others give voice on the trail like the Beagle and the Basset. Also, there is the Dachshund, equipped for digging and fighting when he goes to ground for the badger.

Working Breeds— For the most part these are large dogs bred to assist man in his work. They pull sleds and carts, perform rescue, serve as watchdogs and police dogs and perform many other specialized tasks according to the purpose for which they were bred.

Terriers— The word Terrier derives from the Latin *Terre* which means earth. Thus Terriers are dogs bred to rout out varmints such as badgers, woodchucks, foxes, weasels and rats. The chief characteristics of all Terrier breeds is their gritty tenacity, courage and devotion to home and family.

Toy Breeds— The Toy Group is composed of very small breeds; hence, the word toy. They usually are less than 10 pounds in weight. They have been household pets for centuries. Many are miniatures of other breeds and although the Toys look frail and fragile they are fairly hardy. They require little exercise, space or food and therefore make excellent pets for apartment dwellers.

Non-Sporting Breeds— This is a miscellaneous collection consisting of breeds that did not fit in exactly with other groups. This varied group has been selectively bred either for esthetic effect, or to perform some precise function.

Herding Group— The Herding group consists of 15 breeds of dogs whose talent and claim to fame is their ability to herd sheep and cattle. Man's use of dogs to help him tend livestock dates from ancient times, and a good herding dog is still prized today. Quickness, stamina and an uncanny intelligence are the marks of the herding dog.

3

Acquiring A Puppy

*The most important part of buying any puppy
is an honest and ethical breeder*

Advantages

Puppies are new molds that you can shape into a sound personality and with whom you can develop a close bond. You can teach them right from the start and keep bad habits from developing. You know where they came from and how they were bred. You can watch them grow.

Disadvantages

Puppies require a lot of care and attention and several weeks or months of housebreaking. You can never be 100% sure how a puppy's personality and habits might turn out. Some puppies are like adolescent children and may be extremely active and mischievous. This developmental stage requires patience. Some puppies may challenge for dominance and you may need to be firm, not harsh, to establish control.

Quality Breeders

A great deal of the success you will have with your dog depends on what happened to the dog **before** you acquired him; its socialization, genetic background and early conditioning are the result of the breeders' efforts. There is no organization or registry that can guarantee the quality of a dog. Technically, anyone who breeds dogs can be considered a breeder. With that in mind it is up to you to do your homework and buy quality.

Types of Breeders

Hobby Breeders- The serious and dedicated hobby breeder regards his dogs as a hobby of love. Hobby breeders do not expect a big profit and may only breed once a year, if that. When someone breeds dogs for the enjoyment, pleasure, and thrill of producing the very finest specimens of the breed, the result is superior quality. These breeders acknowledge responsibility for each and every puppy produced and stand behind every dog they breed.

Commercial Kennel- This breeder has progressed from a hobby breeder who plans one or two litters per year to a large operation that produces many litters per year. This type of breeder adheres to high ethical standards and constantly works to improve his or her line.

Backyard Breeder- This is a person who owns a pet and thinks it would be good income to have puppies. This person knows little about the science of breeding for health and sound temperament and cuts corners in order to make the litter pay off. They may use the closest and cheapest mates, may not provide a proper diet, not give preventative vaccinations, and sell the puppies as soon as they are weaned. They usually deal in the more popular breeds because the puppies will sell quickly and easily.

Accidental Breeder- This is a person whose bitch got caught by the neighbor's dog or they have a litter because they want the kids to witness the birthing process or they may want to pick up some quick money. There is no planning and the bitch may not have received proper care or be of sound reproductive quality.

Puppy Mills- These operators may have a number of bitches of popular breeds they keep in cramped cages or stalls, one or two studs (which may be purchased champions of record), and will breed the bitches every heat period. Sometimes the bitch will never leave her small confined area. Her puppies are usually taken from her as soon as they start to eat solid food. This deprives the puppy of lessons they can only learn from their litter mates and may result in a number of serious temperament problems.

Pet Shop Dealers- This source of acquiring a puppy is difficult to appraise because the standards and practices for each business varies. Pet shop puppies usually come from a variety of different breeders with some being thousands of miles away. Unless there is considerable quality control, such as routine inspections of breeders' facilities and breeding practices, it is difficult to ensure quality.

The fact is you will probably pay the same cost wherever you purchase your puppy. It's up to you to ensure that you get quality.

Ten Things Quality Breeders Do

1   Quality Breeders conscientiously plan each litter based on parents' appropriate temperament, freedom from congenital and hereditary defects, and qualities in relation to the breed's AKC approved official standard. Before deciding to produce a litter, breeders consider the possibilities of properly placing puppies they cannot keep for themselves. A quality breeder breeds only the best dogs or "champions" — a champion is a dog who has proven itself to be an outstanding example of the breed in temperament and structure and is worthy to be bred. Most breeders plan breedings well in advance and may have waiting lists of buyers. Don't expect to call and take "immediate delivery." Most will know of other reputable breeders who have litters or are expecting litters.

2   Quality Breeders verify in writing that the parents have been pronounced normal and that congenital health problems in the breed have been cleared by a veterinarian specializing in the field, or through a national registry such as the Orthopedic Foundation for Animals (OFA), Canine Eye Registry Foundation (CERF) and von Willebrand Disease (VWD). Each dog certified clear is given a certification number (preliminary evaluation is given to dogs under two years). The OFA, CERF certification number of the sire and dam appear on the AKC application for individual registration (blue slip). The OFA, CERF numbers (or a copy of the preliminary OFA evaluation) of the parents will be provided by a quality breeder if the problem exists in the breed. See Health Caution section.

3 Quality breeders take care to plan the spacing of litters so that puppies are not consistently available. The average breeder breeds every one to three years. Quality breeders breed only healthy, mature stock over one and one half years of age. Bitches should have no more than two litters in any 18-month period and no bitch should be bred after the age of eight years. All breeder stock is kept under sanitary conditions and given maximum health protection through worming, inoculation, and proper veterinary care at all times.

4 Quality Breeders register their stock with a national registry and keep accurate records of breedings and a four or five generation pedigree. (A pedigree is a list of each dog's ancestors.)

5 Quality Breeders present the puppy to the new owners no sooner than 7 weeks of age. All new owners are provided with written details on feeding, general care, dates of worming and inoculations and a four-generation pedigree.

6 Quality Breeders screen future owners. They will ask many questions to ensure the puppy will go to a proper home. Quality breeders are concerned about the welfare of their puppies and do not want to create a mismatch which could jeopardize the life of their pups and the reputation of their kennel.

7 Quality Breeders require purchasers to spay and neuter those dogs which for any reason will not be used for breeding, and to properly safeguard unspayed bitches from unplanned matings and most of all, to ensure a healthier animal. Some breeders offer an AKC Limited Registration which means the dog is a pure bred AKC registered dog; however, no offspring of the dog may be registered with the AKC. This ensures that only the best stock is bred. Limited Registration dogs may not be shown in conformation but may be shown in obedience.

8 Quality Breeders will make sure you are aware of the pros and cons of their breed as well as the grooming, shedding and trimming requirements, if any.

9 Quality Breeders are always available to help with any questions or problems that may arise and assume responsibility for every puppy they produce throughout the lifetime of the animal. They care about their breed and are actively involved in rescue work.

10 Quality Breeders usually participate in dog clubs. This indicates depth of involvement. The breeder is exposed to other points of view, learns more about their breed, general dog care, modern breeding practices and is kept up to date. Frequently they will be breeding in accordance with a club "code of ethics."

Buyer Beware   Don't be overly impressed by AKC papers. They are only a birth certificate and do nothing to ensure quality of the puppy or the breeder or the seller.

Seek out a breeder with whom you have confidence.

Visit many breeders, see the mother and other relatives, and see the conditions under which the puppy was raised. A surprising amount of behavior is inherited. Also, the puppy's environment has a great deal to do with his personality. The parents may be one of the best indications of the future temperament of your new puppy.

Do not request a less expensive, pet quality animal from the breeder if you have plans to breed or show.

The buyer should not purchase any purebred animal without AKC registration papers or a written sales agreement specifying condition of sale and a time guarantee. The bill of sale should state breed, sex, and color of dog, date of birth, dog's registered sire and dam names and puppy's litter registration number, if available. Have the breeder sign and date the bill of sale information.

Dog ownership requires commitment. Dogs must be cared for daily, receiving a healthy diet and regular exercise, plus grooming and veterinary attention, including regular inoculations against the major infectious canine diseases.

No puppy should be sold unless it receives at least one vaccination which includes distemper, hepatitis, leptospirosis, and parvo virus. Written proof should be provided stating what vaccines it has received, when and by whom.

If the puppy was dewormed, what was the drug used and when was it given? If the puppy was not dewormed, was a fecal exam done?

Beware of illness; signs of runny nose or eyes, skin sores, dirty ears or fleas. A healthy puppy will have clear, shiny eyes that are free from discharge. Its coat will be glossy with a minimum of flaking skin. It should be alert and playful.

Your primary needs should be to find a breed with a good temperament that is suitable to your household and a dog with sound health. The looks, color and sex of the animal should be secondary.

Don't make buying a dog like buying a car. This is not done on impulse but rather a rational, well-thought-out decision that you will have to live with for 12 to 14 years. If you make a mistake, it could cost the life of the dog you choose. Research the temperament and physical requirement of each breed for compatibility **before** you buy. Be prepared to wait until the right puppy becomes available.

Your puppy should be examined by a vet within 48 hours after purchase and should be checked for general health. If the veterinarian deems the animal unsuitable for reasons of health, the dog should be returned for a second animal or a total refund. Put it in writing!

If paying the price of a show potential/breeding quality animal, provisions should be made in the bill of sale for a refund or replacement animal in the event a show quality dog has disqualifying faults or hereditary diseases.

Quality breeders set a reasonable price for their young puppies. They give first class care and cannot afford to sell at a low price.

4

Puppy Care

Puppy's Equipment

Collect these items together before your puppy arrives:

1. A suitable bed — a basket, box, or a thick lambswool pad.
2. An old blanket or a towel that is soft and easy to clean.
3. Two bowls — one for food the other for water. Look for stoneware or solid metal or stainless steel.
4. A buckle collar and leash (Never use a slip collar (choker) until 5-6 months of age).
5. Dog brush, comb, currycomb, shampoo, flea products and nail clippers (Ask your breeder for type).
6. A dog chew, like a good quality rawhide, and a dog toy that is safe.
7. High quality puppy food.

Additionally, look at the advantages of a good dog crate (It can be a big aid in training), baby gate, seat belt or car restraint, carpet stain and odor remover.

Puppy Proofing = Safety

Eliminate all potential dangers before they become problems.

Remove and safeguard anything that the puppy could chew or swallow that may be of danger such as:

Cleaning compounds, bug sprays, rodent poisons, antifreeze drippings, electrical wires, and mothballs.

Dispose of chicken or turkey bones in a safe manner.

Leave toilet lids down.

Keep upper story windows closed.

Avoid flea collars and dips until 15 weeks of age.

Keep your puppy away from toxic plants.

Check to see the fencing is secure.

TIP Ask your veterinarian when it is permissible for your puppy to be around other dogs.

The First Night Your puppy will benefit from sleeping near you for the first few nights and should be provided with comfort during your absence. A hot water bottle and a blanket should give it some physical comfort. If you don't have a crate, use a cardboard box or basket. A crate provides a simulated den that is portable and useful in training and is highly recommended.

During the first few nights you have to be firm; the puppy has to get used to its sleeping place. If it starts crying and yowling, don't coddle it. After a few nights of disrupted sleep acclimatization will take its natural course. If it starts crying in the middle of the night refer to housebreaking suggestions.

Observe your puppy's routine. Try to establish a routine and stick to it.

A dog is a pack animal. Once you remove your dog from its litter, your dog will look to you for its physical and social needs.

Feeding Puppy Puppies are entirely dependent on their owners to provide a balanced diet that meet all of their nutritional requirements. A dog's nutritional needs change as they grow, so there are different foods for puppies, for mature dogs, for extra-active dogs and older dogs.

Each dog should have the diet that is formulated for his stage of life. Foods designed for puppies are higher in fat (to meet their high energy needs), higher in protein and fortified with vitamins and minerals to enhance growth and development. Feed a puppy a specially formulated puppy food until it reaches maturity (12 to 18 months of age — the larger the dog the longer they take to mature). Any change in diet should be done gradually over a 3 to 5 day span.

General Rule for puppy is feed smaller portions more often:

Weaning time	
3 weeks to 3 months	4 meals a day
3 months to 6 months	3 meals a day
6 months to 1 year	2 meals a day
1 year and up	1 or 2 meals a day (1/2 daily amt if 2)

TIPS Feed your puppy a high-quality, premium dog food. All dogs are individuals and their needs may vary depending on activity, breed and age. Feed for 30 minutes per feeding then remove. Have regular times of the day for feeding. Try not to feed after 6 or 7 pm. Regarding strenuous exercise, allow one hour before and after feeding. The dog should always have clean water available. For puppies less than three months of age, you may prefer to soften their dry food with a little warm water.

Identification Animal Control officials state one of the main reasons for euthanizing is the fact dogs are turned in with no traceable identification. Any dog has the potential to get out and get lost. It is vitally important for your dog to wear a collar with his license number, rabies vaccination tag, and medallion with dog's name (some people include the word REWARD), your name, address and telephone number. Other methods are available, such as tattoos or microchips. See Identification Suppliers in Service Resource Directory Section.

TIP Don't use an S Ring. Use an O Ring. S rings get caught, are easily opened, and the ID gets lost.

Puppy Vaccinations

It is vitally important that you immunize your puppy against infectious diseases that can seriously harm or kill it. Make arrangements with your veterinarian for a vaccination *series* and follow their recommended schedule based on exposure to diseases in your area.

According to the American Veterinary Medical Association, a general schedule is: a puppy's first vaccinations would ideally take place at six to eight weeks, followed by two more vaccinations three to four weeks apart. Afterward, yearly booster vaccines will provide ongoing protection. The most serious life-threatening diseases are distemper, hepatitis, leptospirosis (known as DHL), parainfluenza, parvovirus (known as PP) and rabies. Rabies vaccinations are usually given around four months, with re-vaccination one year later. Three-year immunity vaccines are available. Bordetella and coronavirus vaccine may also be recommended by your veterinarian depending on exposure. It is the law that all dogs must have rabies vaccinations.

Ten Do's & Don'ts for Children's Safety

1   Don't approach dogs you don't know without the permission of the adult owner.
    Not all dogs are friendly and some may bite.

2   If an adult tells you it's ok to pet their dog...
    Do not run toward the dog.
    Do not hug, poke, grab or pound on the dog's head.
    Do approach slowly and quietly.
    Do allow the dog to sniff your hand first.
    Do pet the dog gently under his chin or on his chest.

3   Do not touch or pet any dog that growls, snarls or runs away from you.

4   Do not play roughly with any dog.

5   Do not put your hands through fences, car windows, or cages where dogs are.

6   Do not attempt to take bones, food or toys from a strange dog.

7   Do not frighten or startle any dog, especially when it is sleeping.

8   Do not attempt to punish a dog in any way.

9   If an aggressive dog you don't know comes up to you...

   Do not run or yell.

   Do not look directly at him.

   Do stand perfectly still.

   Do watch the dog out of the corner of your eye.

   Do walk away slowly after a minute or two.

10   Do treat all dogs, cats and other animals kindly.

5

Puppy Training

Establishing Leadership

If you've ever watched a young litter of pups at play, you'll recall the pups jumped at and nipped one another. Some were pushier than others. What you observed was the forming of a pecking order. Having evolved from the wolf (a pack animal) the pups instinctively know that a hierarchy, for the survival and safety of the pack, must be established. When the new pup is brought into a human household the instinct does not change. You must take over as leader and teach the pup he falls below humans in his new pack. The pup will accept and be comfortable with the lowest position as long as you are a kind, strong, firm and consistent leader.

To establish leadership there are some rules that must be followed:

Nothing in life is free. Anything your pup wants or needs must be earned by obeying a command (sit).

This is difficult because it is natural for us to give our dogs food, petting, attention, etc. without thinking about it. However, this indiscriminate attention sends the dog the message that he is a dominant member of the "pack." A dog that perceives himself as dominant over you is certainly not going to be easily trained and may cause you some serious problems.

Give your dog one 15-minute down/stay per day

Make sure you are always in a position to follow through. When you give your dog a command or correct him for anything you must be able to enforce what you say. If you tell him to sit and he chooses not to, you must immediately place him in a sit. If you do not, you have effectively taught him that your command means nothing.

Leaders eat first. Feed your dog after you eat.

Leaders enter and exit a door first. Use a leash or command to have your dog wait until you invite your dog to follow out the door.

Create an environment for success. Use your voice and body language effectively. The tone of your voice is more important than words. Say it as if you mean it, and then, if necessary, follow through. Avoid whining or pleading with your dog.

Do not hit your dog as a means of control. This teaches the dog to fear and retaliate. Build leadership by nonconfrontational means only.

There will be a great sense of security instilled in your dog knowing that you are firmly in control.

How to Discipline

You must teach your puppy what is, and what is not, acceptable. To make it easy for both you and your dog remember:

1. Prevent negative behaviors from occurring and reinforce positive behaviors.
2. Never use your hands as weapons.
3. Be consistent.
4. Use a drag line while supervising the dog.
5. Use your voice. Low guttural sounds tend to be effective.
6. Never discipline after the fact.
7. Praise is a motivator. Use a happy, high pitched voice when praising.
8. Tone of voice is very important. Commands tones should be given in a happy, high pitched voice when you want your dog to

move. Use a firm, low voice when you want your dog to stay.

Puppy Training Classes

The earlier you start working with your dog the better. It is important that positive associations and impressions be made with people, places and things in their environment and with humans and other dogs. Your puppy should receive temperament training that is designed to build its confidence and *prevent* future behavior problems, while inhibiting and channeling the biting instinct into more positive outlets.

The best time for puppy class is between 10 and 18 weeks and after the second vaccination. The class situation should be a sterile environment to guard against infectious disease. Consult with your veterinarian.

TIP Do not use a training collar (choke collar) until after the age of five-and-a-half months.

Training with Food

Food is used as a lure/reward in the early stages of training. Trainers use food to lure the dogs into proper position and direct the dogs movements without unnecessary pulling, tugging, yanking or leash jerking. Food is used to convey to the dog the trainer's pleasure in its behavior and at the same time reward it for performance. The best part of using food as a training aid lies in its ability to reinforce positive behavior, motivate your dog to enjoy working for you and reduce the stress inherent in training. Other reward methods are verbal praise, petting or stroking, attention and play.

TIPS Use small tidbits (about the size of M&M's).

Give the treat at the *exact* moment the desired behavior occurs.

Always couple food rewards with verbal praise and/or petting.

Food rewards work best when the dog is hungry.

Don't overfeed with treats. Figure out your dog's daily caloric needs and use part of that for training.

Eliminating the Food Reward

Make sure your dog has a good understanding of the exercises before phase out. Rewards should be given on a random basis (like a slot machine). Start reducing the frequency of the reward slowly over a period of weeks.

Training Equipment

Medium link steel or nylon slip collar for dogs over the age of 20 weeks, otherwise a buckle collar.

A 4-foot to 6-foot leather or nylon leash.

A 20-foot to 30-foot nylon long line.

Soft food treats cut to the size of an M&M.

Safe toy.

Sit

There are two ways to teach the sit command, either using food as a lure/reward, or physically placing your dog in the sit position.

The food method — start by placing the dog in front of you, holding a piece of food or other lure just above your dog's nose (not too high or this will cause the dog to jump). Slowly bring the food back towards the tail and give the single command "Sit." It may be necessary to place your hand behind the pup to prevent rear movement. At the precise second the pup sits, praise him using a happy, high-pitched voice and give him the small food treat. Release him with your chosen release word. Repeat.

The physical placement method — start by placing your puppy at your left side facing the same direction. Place the puppy in the sit position by pulling up on the collar while gently tucking your hand behind the pup's knees. As the rump hits the ground say, "Sit." Praise your dog then release him using a release word. Repeat!

For adult dogs, give the command "Sit" at the same time gently pull up on the leash with your right hand while gently pushing down on his rear with your left hand. The instant he sits praise using a high, happy voice then release him with your release word. Repeat.

The Release Word

Choose a word such as okay, free, break, up, etc., and use the word consistently to release the dog from commands. Praise should not be used as a release.

Sit/Stay

Place your dog in a sit. As you give the verbal command "Stay." Also, give a hand signal by bringing your left hand, palm open, down towards the dog's face. The command must be in a firm voice. If your dog stays in place for just a few seconds, release him. Gradually lengthen the time and build on success. If the dog attempts to get up, verbally correct "No, Sit" and immediately place the dog back into position. Release and praise. Puppies have short attention spans. Don't demand a long stay from them.

Down

Start with the dog sitting on your left and kneel next to him. Rest your left hand on the dog's shoulder and with your right hand, hold a piece of food or other lure above your dog's nose. As you give the verbal command "Down" slowly bring the lure straight down under the dog's chest to the dog's toes. The instant the dog lies down, praise him and give him the treat.

Stand

Give the verbal command "Stand." Place your left hand just in front of the upper part of your dog's rear legs to stop the forward movement. With your right hand hold a lure at the dog's nose or gently pull outward on the leash keeping the leash level to the dog.

27

Dog Owners Guide

Recall

Attach a long line to the pup's collar. While a helper gently restrains the pup by the chest, show him you have a piece of food and then move about twelve feet away. Call your pup by his name followed by the command "Come." Backpedal or turn and run away from your dog. When your dog reaches you, stop and face him and reward him with lots of praise and a treat.

Make a fun game out of it. Gradually work at a greater distance and around distractions. Avoid at all costs doing anything negative when practicing the recall.

Step on the Leash

This exercise is used as a means of establishing leadership and control. (Do not use on puppies under 12 weeks of age.) With a leash attached to your dog's buckle collar, step on the leash close to the snap. This puts your dog in a position where it is uncomfortable to sit or stand.

If your dog struggles or resists lying down, let him. **DO NOT** discipline, look at, talk to, or touch the dog. As your dog learns to accept the position, slowly move your foot up the leash a few inches from the snap to allow head movement. If your dog attempts to stand, move your foot back close to the snap. To release, simply step off the leash. Do not use a release word, pet or praise. Begin the exercise during quiet times for a few minutes, a few time each day. Gradually increase the time. Use the exercise for control at the veterinary office, during dinner time, etc.

Settle

Your pup must learn to lie still for you when you require it. This serves two purposes:
• Establishes leadership by requiring cooperation.
• Prepares the way for teaching the pup to accept routine handling.

To teach your dog this exercise start by placing the pup gently on his side with his head on the floor. Use the word "Settle" in a firm tone.

Require the pup to lie still for a few seconds then release him with your release word. Most pups will put up at least some resistance to this. Use your voice and hands effectively. At the first signs of resistance, correct in a firm tone and physically place. Follow with praise and *slow* stroking, then release.

Walking on the Leash

A positive association with the leash must be made so that the puppy will not perceive the leash as a shackle.

To accomplish this, let the puppy wear the leash around the home on a *buckle* collar while supervised. Do this in a spirit of play for short intervals. Once the pup accepts the leash dragging along, pick up the end and follow him. Proceed to encourage the pup to follow you. Walk at a fast pace with the least amount of pressure on the leash as possible. Praise the dog for walking along nicely. If the dog pulls or becomes distracted, turn and walk briskly in the opposite direction the dog is going. When he catches up to you, praise him in a happy, high-pitched voice. Another way is to simply stop when your dog pulls on the leash and continue after the leash slackens.

Remember the Four P's

Dogs love to learn. Training your dog helps you gain control and gives you the ability to communicate what is expected so that your dog can live harmoniously in your home. In teaching dogs, leadership and authority is the secret of success. You must establish your authority and leadership and communicate with your dog in a positive manner. Never hit! The four P's of training are Patience, Persistence, Practice and lots of Praise.

TIP If you learn when and how to praise effectively and appropriately correct your dog you will have at your fingertips the primary means of communication with your pet. Praise is the language of dogs — and people.

Basic Obedience Classes

Every dog should know basic commands such as *sit, stay, down, stand, heel* and *come.* Your dog should also learn the meaning of *no* and *ok* and be taught not to pull on the leash. Your dog should be able to do this in any circumstance or situation, not just at home. A training class will provide a place of learning in a distracting environment. Take a class and choose a trainer who emphasizes the use of positive reinforcement such as verbal praise, play or treats. You should look for a class where the instructor teaches not only basic commands but dog behavior as well.

Choosing a Trainer

For the first-time dog owner, there is nothing more important than choosing the right instructor to help you through the training process. You need to decide exactly what you want to train your dog to do. Do you want your dog to be a well-behaved companion or do you want to obtain an obedience or conformation title?

Look for a trainer who specializes in a given area. All dogs and dog owners can improve their relationship with basic dog obedience training. The biggest difference in trainers is the use of corrections. Some trainers teach emphasizing positive reinforcement methods using praise and food while others use various forms of coercion with various intensity. Meaning and relevance should be understood by the dog before anyone ever thinks of force or punishment. Positive training and motivational methods place a minimum amount of *stress* on the dog.

The best method of finding someone is word-of-mouth. A good trainer will have an excellent reputation. Select two or three well-referred trainers and ask them the following questions.

Ten Questions You Should Ask a Potential Trainer

1   How do you correct a dog?
2   What methods do you use?
3   Do you use compulsion? If so, how severe?
4   How would you deal with an aggressive dog?
5   How would you train (your breed)?

6   Do you use prong collars, shock collars, choke collars, head harnesses, nylon slip collars or buckle collars?

7   Do you use dominance techniques? Explain.

8   How long have you been in business?

9   How many students are in your classes?

10 Ask if you can monitor a class, and if you can, observe how the trainer works with the students.

Does the trainer explain carefully what is going on, what to expect, and how to do it? Does each student get the attention needed? Are the trainer's methods humane?

Remember, trainers train people to train their dogs. A trainer should have good communication skills. There are many trainers who know a lot about dogs but have a hard time communicating their knowledge. Dog training is both an art and a science that requires using the proper technique for a particular dog temperament. The object of training is to establish a better relationship with your dog. Commands are not an end in themselves, but a means to bring about a better companion dog.

Training Tips for Your Puppy...

Reinforce your puppy with praise and a small piece of food when it urinates or defecates outside in the designated area. Make all desirable behaviors rewarding to your dog through the use of praise, petting, food, etc.

Never punish your puppy if it makes a mistake. Don't rub its nose in it or hit it with a newspaper. If it makes a mistake indoors, clean the area thoroughly with a 50/50 solution of vinegar and water. Don't use ammonia. When dogs urinate they establish a "scent post." It is important that your clean-up removes all trace of odor.

Don't give your puppy unsupervised freedom indoors and avoid leaving unattended outdoors for more than a few minutes. This prevents undesirable behaviors from becoming habits. You can not train a dog you are not with.

Provide a peaceful "safe place" where your puppy can sleep and relax.

Try to develop a routine for eating, walks, play and bedtime.

Even with the most well-behaved dog, there will be some unpleasant moments. Be patient and work to correct your new pet's bad habits.

Don't use a training collar until the dog is between five and six months of age.

Avoid confrontational games such as tug-of-war and wrestling.

Proper discipline begins with the lowest level necessary to get the message across. Never hit or strike your dog in any way. Physical discipline seldom solves behavior problems and, in fact, frequently causes some very serious problems. For a number of reasons, punishment is an ineffective and often counterproductive method of changing behavior. A far better approach to obtaining good behavior from your dog is to *prevent* inappropriate behavior and train and reward appropriate behavior.

Training Tips for all Dogs...

Dogs must have a clear idea of what it is you want them to do, and the meaning of the command before any correction is administered.

Because everything your dog does is rewarding in some way, allowing undesirable behaviors to occur is the same as training it.

Dogs live in the "here and now." Corrections or positive reinforcement must occur as the behavior is exhibited. A delay of even two seconds reduces effectiveness. After the fact punishments are to be avoided.

Do not give any command that you are not in a position to physically require should the command be ignored. Give the command in a firm voice but do not repeat a command that is not obeyed. Instead, immediately require the behavior. For instance, if a sit command is ignored, place the dog in a sit. Follow with praise even though you physically required the sit.

Consistency is essential. If there is no clearcut rule, the only possible result is confusion and inappropriate behavior.

In order to build reliability, it is necessary to train in multiple locations. Begin with conditions that present very low levels of distraction, like a hallway or room. Once the exercises are successful, proceed to more distractive conditions. (Dogs are excited by movement.)

Dogs learn best by working for a few minutes at a time, several times per day if possible.

Be firm and exacting in your training sessions but keep them lively and fun. Finish each session on a positive note and follow with a brief play period.

Be prepared for occasional "bad days." Dogs have them too!

Dog Behaviorists

Dog Behaviorists are people who study the way dogs act and react to their environment by taking into account the dog's evolutionary development. Behaviorists try to convey in everyday language why dogs behave a certain way in certain situations and how you can use this knowledge to make life with your dog as rewarding as possible.

6

Preventing Behavior Problems

Starting Off "The Right Way"

Fact — Puppies are extremely social animals. The socialization that occurs in a pup's or adolescent dog's life could be the most influential factor in determining how successfully and happily he will relate to his environment. The dog owner holds the key to this important process.

Begin early. The most important socialization period is from 3 to 12 weeks of age. Dogs that are isolated during these critical weeks may become fearful and/or aggressive and are unable, during the entire course of their lives, to handle new people or normal situations. Provide contact with as many different types of people as possible — men, women, children, teenagers, oldsters and quiet or loud people, as soon as your dog has received its vaccinations against disease. Expose him to parks, shopping centers, school yards. Avoid isolating him in yards.

Enroll in a puppy or beginner obedience class. A good program stresses control through positive reinforcement and *nonconfrontational* leadership techniques. These approaches benefit the dog by building confidence and trust as well as controlled exposure to other people and dogs.

Reinforce confident behavior. If your dog shows any concern or aggressive behavior in any circumstance, do not draw attention to the situation by attempting to soothe, calm or console him with sympathetic tones or petting. Doing so rewards him for the behavior. Corrections can be reinforcing or counterproductive. Instead, reward your dog by praising and petting when he shows calm or positive responses to people or noises. Lead your dog into potentially fearful situations with confidence. If you are tentative and nervous, your dog will sense this. Your abilities to successfully send appropriate signals will be enhanced by establishing leadership over your pup. If you see any sign of fearfulness or fear-related aggression, begin working with it immediately. Dogs do not "outgrow" such problems. In fact, if left untreated, they worsen. A fearful animal needs exposure but it must be *carefully controlled* to avoid making the problem worse. A dog's behavior can be complex, and treatment may require the expertise of a behaviorist.

Puppy Socialization & Development

Fact — Less than 30% of family dogs remain with one owner their entire life. A majority are given up because the owner could not deal effectively with problems stemming from puppyhood like chewing, barking, house-soiling, etc.

One of the most important qualities of a pet dog is its temperament. A dog with a good temperament is a joy to own, whereas an aggressive, antisocial, fearful or untrained dog can be a nightmare. A dog's temperament is much more adaptable than is commonly thought and it is greatly affected by the process of training and socialization that occurs during puppyhood. In many ways puppyhood is the most important time of a dog's life, a time when experiences are new and have a longlasting effect on shaping the dog's future personality.

Dog owners should pay heed to this crucial period in the life of their dog, since this is the most important time to influence the proper development of their pet's behavior. It is much, much easier to prevent problems from developing than it is to attempt to cure them once they have become firmly entrenched. According to Ian Dunn, in the world of domestic dogs, the puppy is usually removed from its natural sources of information at about eight weeks and in most cases finds itself the only dog in a human "den." At eight weeks the puppy is not prepared to deal with the world at large. It thus becomes a human responsibility to continue the pup's education. Failure to do so results in the puppy's inability to adapt to its environment, or at least to adapt in a harmonious way with its human pack members. Enrolling your dog in puppy class will stimulate the puppy's learning, develop his potential, help socialize him with other people and other dogs and give the dog/ owner relationship a chance to fully develop.

Housebreaking   The goal is to teach the puppy to eliminate outdoors and give you a sign that it needs to go out.
The Keys
    Establish a Routine
    Reward Success
    Supervise
    Never Correct or Punish after the Fact
    Deodorize Mistakes

The normal healthy puppy will want to relieve himself when he wakes up, after each feeding, following strenuous exercise or after any excitement. The objective is regularly scheduled daily feeding and walking. Use a crate or confine your puppy to a safe area when you are unable to supervise. Remember, you cannot train a dog that you are not with. Don't let your dog run unsupervised. Look for signs that the dog has to go, such as sniffing, whining, turning in circles or going to the door. Place your dog on the leash and take him to his spot. Praise him for successful achievement. Teach your puppy to perform on command. Use short words like, "Hurry up." Praise him for successful achievement. Set a time limit of three to five minutes. If a puppy does not do his business by then, put him back in a confined area. Repeat the process in ten minutes.

Any excitement, such as play, may result in floor wetting. When an accident happens, never punish after the fact, especially by striking with a newspaper or rubbing his nose in it. Thoroughly deodorize the entire stained area with an odor neutralizer. The only effective correction is to catch the dog in the act. If you see the dog about to eliminate make a loud noise by banging on a wall or counter; when they stop, say "outside" and immediately take them to their spot outside. You must make it clear to the dog that it is not the act of elimination that you are displeased with, it is the location.

A puppy cannot effectively control its elimination until approximately five to six months. A young pup's bladder is not mature enough to go through the night without relieving itself. Take the pup out before you go to bed and then confine the pup to a small area like a crate where it is comfortable and able to stand up and turn around. When you hear the pup become restless, get up and take it out. If you are a heavy sleeper, you will need to set your alarm for four to six hours after retiring. A puppy should hold it through the night around four to five months.

Note: A crate is strongly recommended.

Crate Training

Crate + Dog = Happy Home

Crates simulate a den. A den to a dog is a place that provides protection from predators and the elements, a place where he or she feels safe and secure. The use of a crate can help prevent housebreaking and chewing problems. Here is how to crate train:

First, form positive associations with the crate by tossing in dog treats or feeding your dog in the crate *without* closing the door.

DON'T FORCE HIM. Let him take it slowly. He may be shy at first.

Once he is accustomed and unafraid, make him stay in the crate by restraining him at the door with your hand for a few minutes. Gradually increase the time. Make sure you praise him!

Once he is comfortable with this, restrain him with the door while using praise. Eventually, the pup will sit quietly and sleep with the door closed.

Do not always leave the house when you place your dog in the crate (you don't want your dog to associate your leaving with being in the crate).

Don't release your dog from the crate when it barks, only when it is quiet.

If you are going to be gone for an extended time, arrange for someone to let your dog out.

Don't use housebreaking pads inside the crate. Never punish your pup by putting him in the crate.

Place the crate in an area where the pup can see family activity.

Keep your pup in the crate during all unsupervised short intervals (not more than 3 to 4 hours except night time sleeping). For longer periods, use a puppy pen.

Most young pups have to go every 2-4 hours. At 5-6 months, a dog can usually "hold-it" longer.

If you can, let a new puppy sleep in your room in a crate.

Puppy Nipping or Biting

Mouthing and nipping at hands and clothing is a natural puppy behavior although it is unacceptable to the family. Puppy teeth are sharp and can hurt human skin and tear clothing. The nipping has absolutely nothing to do with teething. Your pup will nip as a means of controlling you to see where he falls in the hierarchy of his new human pack.

Never use your hands to discipline your pup for mouthing. Avoid slapping, squeezing or holding the mouth shut or shaking the dog and pinning it down. All of these ways may teach the pup your hands are weapons and he needs to defend himself when he sees them. Using your hands negatively towards the pup may also teach fear, confusion and mistrust. A good strong leader never has to use force to get compliance. Remember to praise your pup for all appropriate behavior including *light* mouthing. Use chew toys to redirect the pup's nipping. This will be most successful if you distract and redirect as the pup is *about* to misbehave. If the nipping is too hard a loud firm UUUH! should temporarily stop the pup. Immediately praise if pup stops.

A dog generally will not respect leadership in a child. Your pup will view your children as litter mates. Play between children and dog should be supervised by adults. No roughhousing, chasing or wrestling games. This encourages the pup to be more oral and fight against you. Children may use a sharp yip sound to stop the pup then an adult should take over.

As always, make sure the pup is getting plenty of exercise to expend some of his energy.

Due to the age they were removed from their litter or personality, some puppies are mouthier than others. Positive obedience training is recommended so the pup will learn what is expected. If you're having trouble controlling your pup, seek the help of a professional trainer or behaviorist.

Chewing

Dogs chew for many reasons. In puppies, teething is a factor, along with investigation and curiosity. In older dogs chewing may be a means of relieving monotony and or stress. Our goal should not be to stop the dog from chewing but to channel the behavior to appropriate objects. We believe it is important for a dog to have a wide variety of chew objects differing in size, texture and shape. Dogs learn with more variety and stay interested longer.

Providing safe chew toys is step one. To your dog these objects and your remote control or new pair of shoes are all objects to chew. You must teach the dog what is his. Everything else belongs to us. Praise all appropriate chewing. Most owners neglect to do this and fail to take advantage of an easy and pleasant way to avoid undesirable chewing.

Prevent undesirable chewing, (See crate training), especially in your absence. Each time your dog engages in inappropriate chewing and you are not there to correct him for it, he has learned to do it. You have actually trained the behavior by default. Even more importantly, you are risking your dog's life. Allowing a chewer to get a hold of inappropriate objects can be deadly. Poisoning, blockages, punctured intestines, electrocution are just a few of the dire possibilities.

Discipline may be used only when you catch the dog in the act. Clap your hands, toss a magazine near the dog, yell "HEY," or attach a length of light cord or rope to a collar so a sharp "pop" may be given. Praise the dog the second he stops and substitute an acceptable item. Praise the dog for any attention given to the appropriate item.

TIP Tug of war games may cause a dog to become more oral and excitable and are to be avoided. Meal times should be on a consistent schedule to eliminate the possibility of hunger stress. Don't make a big fuss when you leave or arrive. If you find your dog has chewed something inappropriate, don't hit the dog or punish the dog. Put the dog out of sight in a safe place, clean up the mess, count to ten and act like nothing happened. At that time it is too late for any meaningful training to take place.

Chewing problems can be exasperating and costly, however, if you can apply good prevention, correction and reinforcement techniques, most chewing problems can be solved. The help of a professional behaviorist may be required for severe problems.

Digging

There are many reasons for a dog to dig. Some dig cooling pits to lie in, others bury things. Some dig after vermin or as a means of escaping the yard. Many dogs dig out of boredom and frustration or because digging is simply an enjoyable pastime.

A number of things can be done to channel and correct your dog's digging — but there is one familiar rule that must be recognized: you can't train a dog you are not with. A key to solving any problem involves preventing and retraining.

One solution is to create a doggie digging pit, a chosen place where a dog is encouraged to dig. The owner may bury some interesting toys in the pit while the dog watches. The dog is then enthusiastically encouraged to dig them up and is praised. The dog should be confined to the well-stocked digging area when the owner is not present.

This will encourage the habit of digging in the right area. Next, the owner must spend some time in the yard with the dog watching it closely. The dog must be immediately verbally corrected for the beginnings of inappropriate digging and instructed back to the digging pit.

Chicken wire buried at an angle or a strong piece of plywood driven vertically two feet into the ground may discourage digging to escape.

Correcting outdoor behaviors can be much more difficult than training a dog to behave acceptably inside the home.

Remember the dog's social and exercise needs. Are they being met? If not, they may contribute to problem digging and misbehavior. Digging is a natural behavior for a dog. Beware of only taking a corrective approach to the problem. If in doubt about what to do, consult a professional trainer or behaviorist.

Possessiveness (Food and Objects) It is not unusual for a dog to growl or even bite when someone approaches his food dish or prized possession. This is natural response which, in the wild, ensures survival, but in our homes is inappropriate and dangerous. Punishment is not an effective approach and may make matters worse. We must teach our pups that people around his food dish is very positive.

Start announcing chow time by shaking the food bag. Ask your pup to sit and put down his empty dish. Drop two or three pieces of kibble in the dish. After the pup eats them repeat the procedure three or four times. Next, drop some kibble into the bowl. While the pup is eating, offer him a small piece of chicken with your hand next to his bowl, repeat. Now, put more kibble in the dish and while the pup is eating pick up the bowl, add a piece of chicken, give it back to him. Now, while the pup is eating, gently pet him and offer more desirable treats. By practicing this exercise your pup will learn that your hands come to give, not to take away. A trust will develop.

Make sure your pup will relinquish objects to you. Start by pressing firmly but gently at the dog's muzzle directly behind the two canine teeth. The pressure will cause the dog to open his mouth. Now, while he is holding a favorite chew toy press at the muzzle and say "Out" or "Give." When the pup relinquishes the article praise and give it back to him. Repeat the procedure several times with many different objects, always ending the session with the pup keeping the article.

Please note: These exercises are to prevent aggression. If you own a dog that is already exhibiting threatening behavior do not attempt a cure on your own. Seek the help of a qualified behaviorist.

Barking

Barking to a dog is like singing to a canary or talking to a human, a natural normal behavior. This normal behavior may occur at inappropriate times or become too excessive if not controlled by the owner. Barking is a way of communicating a message. Some dogs are more prone to excessive barking than others. This may be due to genetics, early learning or personality.

Some of the most common reasons for barking are:

Barking for attention or reward.

Barking out of boredom or barking to seek companionship.

Barking out of stress, fear or frustration, or because of strong territorial instincts.

It is vital we take advantage of and cultivate a dog's social instincts by making him a part of the family.

Provide a proper diet, quality time, training and an exercise schedule that is convenient. Your dog will look forward to being with you while expending excess energy. Provide mental stimulation as well as physical. Teach your dog tricks and work on obedience commands. Avoid keeping the dog in the yard for long periods of time as this may encourage inappropriate barking.

Teach the dog to distinguish between appropriate and inappropriate barking. This may be accomplished by introducing the dog to regular service people, mail person, utility worker, gardener, etc.

Teach your dog the meaning of "quiet." by putting the barking on cue. For example:

Most dogs bark when a doorbell rings. You may take advantage of this by setting up a training situation. You'll need an assistant.

Assistant quietly goes to your front door. You say:

"Rover, speak!" This is the cue for assistant to ring bell. Dog barks, you say "goooood speak, Rover, goood speak!" Repeat several times.

Now while the dog is barking say "Okay now, Rover, quiet. Quiet, quiet." (say this in a hushed tone while gently cupping dog's muzzle closed). Reward for ceased barking. "Gooood quiet, ...Rover!" Repeat process.

Barking is something that can be controlled. Remember, there is a reason and a reward for every behavior your dog exhibits. If barking has become a problem you may want to consult a professional behaviorist.

Jumping Up

Jumping by dogs is a natural instinctive behavior. When dogs jump on people they are trying to greet and get near the face of their pack members.

Jumping, although natural, is unacceptable to humans and can be dangerous. There is nothing more annoying to some people than to be bounded by an enthusiastic pooch, regardless of its size. Whenever we take something natural (jumping) away from our dogs we must teach an acceptable behavior. Jumping is usually exhibited when a dog first meets people. The best way to stop your dog from jumping is to teach him to sit and stay. There are dozens of things a dog cannot do while sitting and staying. Jumping is one of them. Avoid overexciting your dog when a guest arrives. Ask friends to participate in a simulated training session. Have a friend come to the door. Place your dog in a sit/stay. After a period of time your dog should calm down and assume a normal manner. Be consistent and persistent. Anticipate jumping situations. Have a leash available at all times to use for control.

Another method is to turn your back on the dog when he jumps. Pay no attention to him until he settles down. Also, make sure your dog is spayed or neutered.

**Excitement/
Submissive
Urination**

Dogs that urinate when greeting are exhibiting submissive behavior. Punishing or drawing attention to the behavior will make it worse. The way we greet and interact with the dog must be changed. There are several ways in which owners can greet submissive dogs and minimize the probability of eliciting submissive urination. For instance, the owner can squat down while keeping the upper body straight. Avoid direct eye contact, vigorous petting and speaking in a high or excited voice. Redirecting the pup's attention by tossing a toy or piece of food before greeting will also help. The owner may also teach the pup to sit/stay for greetings and practice in easy situations. Handling the problem in the right way should eliminate the problem.

**The Home
Alone Dog**

Provide early morning and after work exercise.

Provide a safe place for your dog when you are gone. Make sure your home is free from hazards. Use a safe room, a fenced yard, a dog run with shade, etc.

Use positive obedience training to build your dog's confidence and provide quality time.

Make your pet feel comfortable by providing a blanket, soft music, safe toys and a bowl of water.

Break up the day by using pet sitters, doggie day care, neighborhood friends or a responsible neighborhood boy or girl you can trust to let the dog out, take it for a walk and play with it.

Don't make a big fuss over your departures and arrivals.

Establish a routine.

Provide the dog with quality time when you are home.

As a general rule crates should not be used for more than 3 to 4 hours except overnight at which time the dog should be let out in the middle of the night until 6 months of age.

Dogs are social animals and could benefit from the company of another pet.

Use a puppy pen, or cordon off an area that is safe and is easy to clean.

Outside Dogs   Dogs are pack animals and happiest living inside with their family. But some dogs can live outside when necessary if you provide the proper shelter. Dogs need interaction with their family. Many behavior problems stem from backyard boredom.

Ask your breeder if your breed adjusts to outdoor living. Be prepared to move your pet inside when heat or cold become extreme. Make sure your pet can't escape your yard and has shade, plenty of fresh water and regular exercise. Consider a second dog if you must keep your dog outside.

Note: A good puppy training program can help your dog make the adjustment to living indoors.

7

Animal Shelter Adoptions

Advantages
An older dog is more settled, both in appearance and personality.

An older dog is probably housebroken and may have had some obedience training.

You don't have the hassles of puppyhood and the frustration of the adolescent stage.

It's less costly.

You probably would be saving the dog's life.

Disadvantages
As an adult, it may be more difficult to change bad habits — but it can be done.

Older dogs may be resistant to new leadership.

You never know what experiences the dog has had and how it affected its temperament.

The Pet Adoption Process
Dedicated personnel in adoption agencies work hard to place pets in *permanent* homes. Every effort is made to assure that each pet offered for adoption is the kind of pet you would want for your family. Dogs that have apparent health or behavior problems are not put up for adoption.

You will be asked to fill out a questionnaire at many agencies. This questionnaire will help to determine a good match. Most agencies require that you be 18 and you have the consent of your landlord. The screening process is designed to protect dogs and future owners from untenable situations. Adoptions usually include spay or

neuter surgery, vaccinations, and health exami-
nations. You may be required to show verifica-
tion that the pet is allowed at your residence,
proof of residence, and you might be asked to
introduce your other family dog (if applicable)
to make sure they can get along. Fees are around
$50-$75 for dogs. Call your local agency for
their fees and requirements.

**The Second-
Chance Dog**

Adopting a dog from a local shelter is an inex-
pensive way to get a family pet and save a dog's
life, but it's not for everyone.

Shelter dogs may have been spayed or neutered,
vaccinated and examined by a veterinarian. As a
family consider the responsibility of time and
care. Too often families get a dog for the
children with the understanding that the children
will be responsible. What usually happens is the
children are not up to the task and the
responsibility falls on the parents. Determine
who will care for the dog's needs. Consider the
kind of dog you want. Have a general idea about
size, coat, temperament, sex and breed characteristics.

Be reasonable in your expectations. Most dogs
are under stress from their experience in shelters.
They are confined and probably lonely, sur-
rounded by strange noises and people. Most of
these dogs are the consequence of owners who
did not have the time nor the understanding to
deal successfully with their needs, some are
strays but most are victims of circumstance; an
owner who has to move, a landlord who objects,
an owner who dies, a divorce. They are separated from the things they know and need your
patience.

Don't be too discouraged when a simple behavior problem is the reason the dog was aban-
doned. What they need most is to have their confidence built. They need owners who are patient
and who will take the time to work with them.
Bonding won't happen overnight. GIVE IT
TIME!

Questions you should ask when you visit a shelter:

1 Find out why the dog is up for adoption.

2 Does it like children?

3 Has it ever bitten anyone?

4 Is it housebroken?

5 Was it an inside or outside dog?

6 Does it require any special care?

7 Does it respond to obedience commands?

8 Is it shy or fearful?

9 Does it bark aggressively, growl or raise its hackles around you or other dogs?

Visit the shelter during the week when shelter personnel have more time. Ask them for their insights. Shelter workers and volunteers are concerned with creating the right match for permanent placements.

Many shelters have quiet areas where you can get to know the pet better. Take a ball and some treats and see how the dog responds to you and the family. Don't be surprised if the dog is frisky, jumps up on you or pulls on the leash. Dogs act out of character in kennel situations. They will probably be excited from being out of the kennel and with people.

TIPS If a dog is affectionate towards you, don't worry too much about why it's there.

Make sure the dog is in good health, with clear eyes, shiny coat, pink gums and tongue. Most veterinarians offer FREE exams for rescued animals.

Homecoming for your Adopted Dog

When you get home, your new family member may be shy, confused and disoriented. He may jump on your furniture, urinate indoors, or show a number of signs of bad manners. Don't worry, with time, patience, persistence and understanding he will soon get the message and know what is expected of him.

51

Treat your new pet as if it were never house-broken. Go back to basics. Establish a routine. Give your dog 6 to 12 weeks to adjust to its new home. Begin by *preventing* problems from occurring by dog-proofing your home and confining your dog to a safe area (with plenty of water) when you are not able to supervise. At first, do not leave your new dog in the company of children unchaperoned. Children can play rough with a dog and be inconsiderate. Spend as much time as you can with your new companion. Build the dog's confidence with basic obedience that uses positive reinforcement methods (praise, treats, petting, play, etc.). Dogs need to know where they fall in the hierarchy; they need activity, regular exercise, a good balanced diet and the companionship of their owner(s). Give the dog attention, but allow him personal space. Never correct after the fact. Never hit your dog or use your hands as weapons. Never yell at your dog. A kind, firm, patient approach will prove successful in the end. For best results seek the help of a reputable trainer or behaviorist who uses positive methods.

Separation Anxiety — a Common Problem

A lot of rescue dogs exhibit "Separation Anxiety" which means the dogs cannot emotionally cope with the absence of their owners. They manifest their anxiety by vocalization (barking, whining, etc.), destructive behavior, escaping, housesoiling, and, in some severe cases, self-mutilation.

NEVER CORRECT or PUNISH a dog that exhibits separation anxiety. When you come home and punish your dog for something he did earlier, he is likely to associate the punishment with his enthusiastic greeting. Therefore, punishment only increases his anxiety. Focus on the positive and reward using verbal praise, treats, petting, etc.

Don't make a big fuss over your departures and arrivals. No *long* affectionate greetings or goodbyes.

Use obedience commands like *sit/stay* to build the dog's confidence.

Use mock departures of varying duration (from 1 minute to 10 minutes), use different stimuli such as grabbing your keys, starting your car, etc.

Use pet sitters, doggie day care, neighborhood friends or a teenage boy or girl who can be trusted to play, exercise and let the dog out during the day.

Taking on a shelter dog with a past is not easy. Only you know if you have the patience and understanding to work through difficulties. Things may proceed slowly, but, if you are committed, the rewards of reclaiming a life can be immeasurable.

Of the people who adopt shelter animals, 79% take home pets younger than 6 months of age, according to the Humane Society of the United States.

A Second Dog The main thing to think about when considering a second dog is space and combinations of dominant or submissive personalities. Will there be enough space for each dog to have a retreat?

If the newcomer is a puppy, the adjustment is usually smooth. If the newcomer is fully grown, you have to proceed with more caution. An ideal combination is a neutered male and a spayed female. Trickier are two bitches, because they often don't get along. More difficult is two males, because sooner or later they will try to establish dominance by fighting. Neutered males are easier. Try to determine if the breed profile suggests dog dominance. Avoid the combination of two dominant dogs or dogs whose breed tends to be aggressive toward other dogs.

TIPS Introduce new dogs outside on neutral ground to avoid initial territorial disputes. Use positive reinforcement. Give adult dogs some quiet time away from the new puppy and some individual attention.

53

Introducing a New Dog to...

**Another
Family Dog**

Introduce dogs on loose leashes in a neutral area. The dogs will use their body language to establish hierarchy. Maintain loose leashes at all times. Some may play bow and romp around together. Give verbal praise to older dogs for positive behavior. If you can, take the dogs for a walk together.

Use a happy, positive tone of voice to show you are pleased with any positive behavior. If you decide to adopt, when you return home let the dogs run around together in your back yard while dragging a leash that is connected to a buckle collar, and let them settle any differences themselves unless they threaten life and limb. When it is time to go inside introduce your new dog to your home while still on leash. Make sure you do not show partiality. Feed both at the same time and in separate food dishes.

An Infant

Most dogs are curious about infants. They should adapt quickly and easily to the presence of a new baby. Since the consequences of a problem can be severe you should observe safety precautions. A baby could be accidently hurt when a dog becomes excited and cannot be controlled. Before your child arrives home, teach your dog obedience commands to control it in exciting situations.

When you bring your baby home, greet the dog without the baby present. Allow the dog to sniff the smell of the baby on you or an article of clothing.

After the excitement has decreased and the dog appears relaxed, gradually introduce the baby. The dog should be on leash, one parent attending to the dog, the other the baby. Place your dog in a sit/stay position approximately 10 to 15 feet from the baby. If the dog appears calm and under control, slowly bring the baby to the dog and allow the dog to sniff (at a safe distance). Reward the dog.

Canine Health & Care

Healthy Signs

Skin should be smooth, flexible and free of scales, scabs, growths or areas of redness.

Coat should be glossy and pliable, without dandruff or areas of baldness. There should be no external parasites or mats.

Eyes should be bright and shiny, free from excessive watering or discharge.

Ears should be light pink, clean with a small trace of wax.

Nose is usually cold and moist.

Temperature is normally 100 to 102.5 degrees (average 101.3).

Gums should appear pink, firm and pigmented.

Teeth should be clean and free of tartar. Breath should be odor free.

Pulse is 70 to 130 beats per minute at rest.

Stools should be firm and free of parasites.

Exercise

One of the most important things you can do for the mental and physical health of your dog is to provide regular exercise.

As a general rule, a twenty- to thirty-minute walk twice a day is sufficient. Dogs are most energetic in the morning. Regularly scheduled walks and runs will help vent a lot of energy that, if pent up for long, can manifest itself in problem behaviors.

TIP Teach your dog to retrieve. If you throw a ball, your dog will search, run after it, and bring it back with great pleasure. Start at an early age and make it exciting. Praise your dog when it successfully retrieves.

Spaying & Neutering

Ten million healthy, friendly dogs and cats will be euthanized in the United States this year simply because they are unwanted. Neutering your dog or cat will not only help control the over-population problem but help to prevent health problems, such as tumors and cancer.

Spaying your female dog won't alter her temperament; however, neutering a male dog will make it a better-behaved pet. To prevent unwanted pregnancies, make this decision at an early age (well before the first heat cycle in female dogs). Consult with your veterinarian.

Spay/ Neuter Facts vs. Myths

Myth It is wrong to deprive an animal of the natural right to reproduce.

Fact There is no physical or behavioral benefit for a dog to bear or sire a litter. A neutered dog will feel no sense of denial or lack of fulfillment.

Myth Neutering will change my pet's personality.

Fact You will benefit by any personality change. Neutered pets tend to be calmer, more contented animals. Males are less likely to engage in several undesirable behaviors including mounting, urine marking in the house, roaming and aggression towards other male dogs.

Myth Neutering my pet will make him fat and lazy.

Fact Too much food and too little exercise lead to obesity.

Myth My dog will become a wimp.

Fact Hunting and protective territorial instincts are not diminished by neutering.

Did You Know... Spay/neutering your dog will reduce the likelihood of several serious illness, including testicular or ovarian cancer.

Spay/ neutering is the only effective solution to a serious pet overpopulation problem. Many dogs surrendered to animal shelters are the result of accidental breedings, owners who think they can make a quick buck by breeding, or want to teach their kids about reproduction and find they can't place the puppies.

Please have your dog(s) or cats spayed or neutered.

Grooming Every dog should be groomed thoroughly and regularly. The grooming routine includes attention to the coat, teeth, nails, eyes and ears. The time and effort varies depending on your breed. It's up to you to be your dog's best friend by looking after his physical needs on a regular basis.

Coat All dogs should be brushed once a day. Not only will your dog be neat and clean but it's a great way to bond with your pet. Dogs love it. First, feel your dog all over for any foreign objects and remove them carefully. Using your recommended brush, hold the hair up a small section at a time and brush downward in short, brisk strokes. When you have done the whole body this way, begin again at the head and use long sweeping strokes to brush in the direction the hair grows to smooth the coat. Make sure you don't pull or hurt the skin. "Plucking" to remove the dead hairs is occasionally necessary for breeds like the terriers. Professional grooming should be used periodically. Consult with your breeder or local club for the kind of equipment you will need.

Bathing Frequent baths remove natural oils and are not good for dogs. Use a shampoo especially formulated for dogs.

Pads & Nails This area requires special attention. Always check between the dog's toes for dirt and foreign objects and possible hair mats. Nails should be trimmed every month so they just clear the floor. Purchase a specially designed nail trimmer at your pet store. Don't use scissors. Ask your groomer or veterinarian to show you how. A dog's nails are sensitive, and the nails should not be clipped too far back.

Ears At least once a week, dirt, dust, and ear wax should be removed from the ears using a cotton swab dipped in alcohol. Proceed gently, and do not probe deeply. Clean only the outer ear. The inner ear should be cleaned and ear wax removed by a professional. If your dog scratches behind the ears a lot, or keeps shaking its head violently, or both, it may have an inflammation. Do not try to clean out an infected ear; seek the service of your veterinarian.

Eyes Make sure hairs do not rub against the eyeball, and any discharge is removed. If there is any inflammation, reddening, tearing or excessive blinking, your veterinarian should be consulted.

Teeth Dogs develop plaque and tartar just as people do. You should clean your dog's teeth twice a week. Use a regular toothbrush and toothpaste formulated for dogs, or salt water or a mixture of equal parts of salt and baking soda. Older, hardened deposits should be removed by your veterinarian.

How to Choose a Professional Groomer

In the state of California there are no special government licenses or requirements to become a groomer. It is important that you know as much as possible about the person to whom you are about to entrust your dog. How long have they been grooming? How did they learn to groom? Ask your veterinarian whom they refer.

Visit the grooming shop before you make your first appointment. Is the shop clean and sanitized? How are the other dogs being treated? Will your dog be in contact with other animals? Is your groomer certified? What shampoo is being used on your pet? What flea-killing agent?

What drying techniques? When practiced properly, grooming should be an enjoyable experience. Look for signs of mishandling when you pick up your dog. Is your dog frightened or timid? Notice how your dog reacts toward the groomer. The Southern California Professional Groomers Association states "when you pick up your dog you should expect nails trimmed, ear hair removed, ears swabbed clean, tummy and pads shaved, dog trimmed according to breed standard, correct shampoo for skin type, and a warning to any noticeable problems." The National Dog Groomers Association of America sets standards and service guidelines for its members, as well as conducts certification programs.

TIP: When you pick up your pet make sure your pet is wearing its own ID tag. Give your dog praise and attention when you pick it up. This helps create a positive association with the grooming experience.

Tick Removal

Ticks should be swabbed with alcohol or a special tick solution and then pulled out slowly with tweezers. You must be careful to remove the blood-sucking parasite completely, including the head and biting parts; otherwise sores and infection may develop.

Nutrition

Part of being a responsible pet owner is providing your dog with a nutritious diet. Throughout its life your pet should be fed a nutritionally balanced food specifically formulated for its age (Puppy, Maintenance, Performance and Senior are the most common stages) and life-style.

Examine your dog's physical condition regularly. Are the eyes clear? Is the coat shiny? Is there dandruff? Are the gums and tongue pink? Are the stools watery or abnormal? Does the animal eat and defecate regularly? Is your dog lethargic? If the answer is yes, consult with your veterinarian to determine a diet that is right for your dog.

The following are a few basic rules of nutrition.

Choose a premium quality food found in pet food stores, animal feed stores or veterinary offices. Quality ingredients in the food cost the manufacturer more and therefore cost you more, but the food is easily digested and has a higher percentage of nutrients that are absorbed in the dog's system. The food is more concentrated, so you don't have to feed quite as much as you would a cheaper dog food to meet your dog's daily nutritional requirements. In the long run, it costs you less.

The basic building blocks of canine nutrition, Protein, Fat, Carbohydrates, Vitamins and Minerals, must exist in *"proper balance"* formulated for the life stage and activity level of your dog.

Calcium/phosphorus ratio levels must be maintained within a range of 1.2% calcium to 1% phosphorus, no more, no less. Zinc is an important mineral that must be included in diets. You can do considerable harm by feeding homemade diets that are nutritionally incomplete.

Dogs, unlike people, do not need variety in their diets.

Labels must list the ingredients in descending order, along with a guaranteed analysis of the product's protein, fat, fiber and moisture. You should also find a claim about its nutritional value for a particular life stage. If manufacturers claim high protein on the label, make sure you know the source. The most readily digestible protein for a dog is the white of an egg which is given a Biological Value rating of 1 by nutritionists, followed by: muscle meats-.90; beef-.84; fish-.75; soy-.75; rice-.72; oats-.66; yeast-.63; wheat-.60; and corn-.54. The cost per pound would fall in the same order. Look on the label to determine from what source the protein is derived. Too many vague terms on the labels are still used and allowed by the government which makes it difficult to compare food quality. You need to choose a manufacturer that you can trust.

TIPS Do not feed table scraps, but if you can't resist those pleading eyes, limit table scraps to no more than 10% to 15% of the diet.

Don't give your dog chocolate!

Feed the amount of food necessary to maintain the dog's proper weight and health.

The Association of American Feed Control Officials (AAFCO) has developed protocols for testing dog food based on controlled feedings. To find if your food has met their approval call: 800 851-0769.

Food Formulated for Age

Feed dog food formulated for your dog's age. The following are examples of size and maturity rate.

Toys	up to 15 lbs.	6 months
Small	15-35 lbs.	9 months
Medium	35-55 lbs.	10-15 months
Large	55-100 lbs.	18-20 months
Giant	100-175 lbs.	22 months

Vitamins for Dogs

Never supplement your dog's diet before consulting your veterinarian. Most commercial dog foods are so sound nutritionally that it could be dangerous to supplement them without the advice of a knowledgeable professional who is aware of your pet's individual health status. Excessive amounts of vitamins are toxic, and minerals like calcium and phosphorus must be kept in the correct balance.

Obesity Test

To determine if your dog is obese, place your hands on its rib cage. You should be able to feel the ribs by gentle pressure. If you cannot, your dog is overweight.

Note: Feeding your dog too much is as bad as not feeding your dog enough. Overweight dogs can develop many problems and their lives can be shortened.

Pill Medication

The easiest way is to disguise the pill in their food. Otherwise, tilt your dog's head upward slightly, then place the pill deep into the dog's throat. Quickly remove your hand and after your dog closes his mouth keep his head elevated and rub or blow on its nose. Usually a dog will lick his nose when he has swallowed the pill. Repeat until successful.

Medical Supplies

You may need these items:
Rectal thermometer (Normal temperature is 100.8 to 102.5; average 101.3)
Petroleum jelly
Hydrogen Peroxide for cuts & wounds and to induce vomiting
Sterile gauze pad and adhesive tape (1 inch wide) and cotton balls
A triple antibiotic ointment such as Neosporin or Bacitracin for surface wounds
Charcoal tablets for poisoning
Use as a stretcher, if needed, a flat board or cardboard box, blanket or towel
Toothbrush and dog tooth paste
Tweezers

First Aid

First aid should be practiced in an emergency situation before you can reach a veterinarian. First, call your veterinarian and alert him or her to the situation. If you are uncertain, they can advise you on the phone.

Restraint You may find it necessary to muzzle your dog if it is injured. Place a strong bandage or necktie about 3 feet long over the dog's muzzle, tie a simple knot under the chin, cross the ends, and tie them behind the ears.

Emergency Transportation Place on a large, firm surface like a plywood board. Large towels or blankets are okay if nothing else is available.

Bleeding Stop the bleeding as soon as possible. Use a pressure dressing; a wad of cotton that will normally stop the flow of blood wrapped by gauze to hold it in place. For severe bleeding, a tourniquet may be necessary. Seek a veterinarian immediately. Tourniquets should be loosened every ten minutes and should be used very carefully. Keep him warm and calm, in case of shock. Do not give liquids, in case of internal injuries.

Fractures The affected limb is usually held in an unnatural position. Keep him as still as possible and transport the dog to your veterinarian using a firm surface. Try to keep the limb supported at all times with a cushion.

Poisoning

Symptoms are abdominal pain, trembling and drooling, shallow breathing, convulsions and eventual coma. Seek veterinary care immediately. Try to save any of the substance or packaging that the pet may have eaten.

TIP If a pet is left alone in a garage, make sure all hazardous materials, especially antifreeze is out of reach. Dogs are attracted to the smell and taste of antifreeze.

Keep snail bait and ibuprofen away from dogs.

National Animal Control Poison Center
University of Illinois
24 hour Hotline (Fee)
1 800 548-2423

Poison Control Hotline
800 876-4766 San Diego
800 544-4404 LA

Summer Cautions

Hot Days Make sure your dog has plenty of fresh water, shade and air. Your dog may eat a little less than usual.

Hot Cars Make sure you don't leave your pet in a car during the hot summer months. Temperatures can heat up fast to unbearable and dangerous levels. If you have to take your pet, park in the shade and provide a constant air supply. The best advice is to leave him at home.

Heatstroke Dogs are susceptible to heatstroke. Be mindful of shade and water and excessive activity during hot weather. Take long dog walks early in the morning or early evening. If you think your dog has heat exhaustion, immediately apply cool water with a garden hose and proceed to a veterinarian. When a dog's rectal temperature is 104 or more, the dog is in serious trouble.

Swimming Most dogs love to swim but don't assume your dog knows how. Go into the water with a stick or ball and call your dog. Never frighten your dog or throw him in. Don't let him overdo it. Be careful of strong tides and access to the beach. Many dogs have drowned because they cannot climb up the embankment or concrete wall of the swimming pool. If you have a pool, teach the dog how to use the steps.

Snakebite

Symptoms include swelling, labored breathing, glazed eyes and drooling. Proceed to vet while keeping the dog warm, calm and inactive.

Bee Stings

Sting bites produce pain and swelling. A dog that has a severe reaction needs veterinary attention. An ice cube over the sting will ease the pain and swelling.

Disaster Preparedness and your Dog

Be prepared with:
2 weeks supply of canned and dry pet food
2 weeks supply of bottled water
Flashlights, batteries, candles and radio.
Can opener
Heavy blanket
Set of bowls
Crate
2 leashes per dog
First aid kit and medications
Health records & vaccinations
Photo, in case your dog gets lost
Most important, always keep ID tags on your pet, in addition to your name and number, use a contact number for a person that is out of your area.
Secure all bookcases and cabinets to the wall.
Ask a neighbor, in advance, to care for your dog in the event you are away when disaster strikes.

Have a plan for boarding — know hotels that accept pets, line up a reputable kennel. Red Cross shelters do not accept animals inside their buildings.

Dog Fights

Dogs fight mainly over territory, social hierarchy, or a female in heat. The best advice is to prevent fights before they start. Keep dogs separated. Otherwise, you must act quickly and make sure you don't endanger yourself. Try throwing water on the dogs, if available. After the fight flush open wounds with water and hydrogen peroxide and seek veterinary attention.

How You Might Avoid Being Bitten by a Dog

When Dogs Might Bite

When they feel threatened or afraid.
When they are protecting their territory, food, toys, family or pups.
When they get excited — even in play.
When they don't know you.
When their chase response is triggered.
When they have been bred or trained to be aggressive.
When they are in pain or irritated.

How to tell when a dog may bite

The dog will stand stiff and still, with his hair (hackles) up.
The dog may stare at you.
The dog may hold his tail stiff and up in the air and may wag it back and forth very fast.
The dog may growl, snarl, show teeth, or bark strongly.

What To Do

Stand very still and try to be calm. DON'T SCREAM AND RUN.
Don't stare directly at the dog — but be aware of it.
Don't make any sudden moves.
Try to stay until the dog leaves; if it doesn't very slowly back away.
If the dog comes up to sniff you, don't resist.
If you say anything, speak calmly and firmly.
Plan, in case of attack, to buffer a bite with a purse, jacket or other object.
If you fall or are knocked down, curl into a ball with your arms and hands over your head and neck. Try not to scream or roll around.

If you get bitten, report all bites to police or animal control, seek treatment and remember to give a description to the authorities so they can find the animal and determine if the dog has rabies.

Life Expectancy The length and quality of your dog's life will depend on genetics, nutrition and care. You can't control genetics but you can have an influence on nutrition and care.

Small and medium dogs age fifteen human years their first year then nine years the next year and four years every year from two on. A seven-year-old dog would be 44. Large and giant breeds age 12 years the first human year and 7 years thereafter. A 5-year-old-dog would be 40 in human years.

The Older Dog Dogs are considered in their senior years around the age of eight. About 10% of the dog population is over 10. Our special friends need thoughtful care in order to make their remaining time with us comfortable. Your veterinarian should be consulted as to the best care to prolong the quality of life for your dog. Pay close attention to: feeding and nutrition, grooming and preventive care.

Feeding Activity levels and metabolism rates slow, reducing the amount of calories required. Your dog will need a special diet formulated for older dogs. If you don't make the adjustment your dog can become overweight, hastening illness. An ideal diet would be lower in protein and lower in fat than a normal maintenance diet. The source of protein is important to consider. For best direction consult with your veterinarian. Because older dogs eat less, the diet should be of high quality to supply the necessary daily nutrients. Because digestion and absorption takes longer, try feeding smaller portions more often but no more than their daily caloric requirement.

Prevention Dogs, like people, should have periodic physicals for early detection and treatment. Vaccinations should be up-to-date. Ideal weight should be maintained. Moderate exercise helps to fight obesity and keep the joints supple. Older dogs adjust poorly to physical and emotional stress. They love routine. Special care should be exercised to prevent exposure to extremes in weather and to provide a shelter away from rain, cold and drafts. Make sure your dog's teeth are clean and free of tartar to prevent bad breath, gingivitis and periodontal disease.

Grooming The older dog's coat can get dry and brittle. Skin tumors are more common. Frequent brushings, combined with regular bathing with a specially formulated shampoo recommended by your veterinarian is advised. Toe nails need to be trimmed more often. When wet, your dog should be toweled dry thoroughly and kept in a warm room.

Euthanasia

When life becomes difficult and ceases to be enjoyable, when the dog suffers from a painful condition for which there is no hope of betterment, it is perhaps time to say goodbye.

Death of a Family Pet

As an integral part of the family we are emotionally affected by the loss of our dog. Unfortunately, there are no social rituals like funerals and wakes that act to support us during these troubled times. Society does not offer a grieving pet owner a great deal of sympathy. Still, the loss of a pet affects our emotions and usually progress through several stages. Recognizing them can help us cope with the grief we feel:

Denial The initial response many owners exhibit when faced with their pet's terminal condition or sudden death.

Bargaining typically happens when the individual will try to make a deal to spare the life of their pet.

Anger can be exhibited by hostility and aggression or can turn inward, emerging as guilt. You can get mad at your veterinarian or someone else but you are just relieving frustration at the expense of another. You can also go through a number of "if onlys," i.e., if only I had acted earlier.

Grief is the stage of true sadness. The pet is gone and only emptiness remains. It is important to have the support of family and friends and to talk about your feelings. It is helpful to recognize that other pet owners have experienced similar feelings and that you are not alone in this feeling of grief. See below for helpful hotlines.

Resolution All things must pass — even grieving. As time passes, the distress dissolves as the pet owner remembers the good times, not the passing. Many find the answer lies in giving a good home to a dog in need of a good owner.

The pet loss support Hotlines:

University of California
School of Veterinary Medicine
Davis, California
916 752-7418

The Delta Society
206 226-7357

San Diego County Bereavement Program
619 275-0728

9

Veterinarians

Tips on Choosing a Veterinarian

Look for a veterinarian who will take the time to speak with you, will make the effort to explain any problems in layman's terms and is accessible.

The key word is *confidence*. Look for cleanliness and note how the hospital smells. If you don't feel comfortable being there, chances are neither will your pet.

Is the staff friendly and caring? Do they make you feel comfortable?

What are their hours? Is anyone on duty at night, in case of emergency? Most vets are not open around the clock, but make sure you know where you can go after hours.

All certified veterinarians must have credentials. You should know his or her credentials and their reputation.

Can you take a tour of the facilities? Do they have any special equipment? Are the sick animals isolated from the other animals?

The Puppy Exam

Smart puppy buyers make the sale of their new pet contingent on passing a medical exam by a veterinarian. This initial exam consists of a check for detectable birth defects that could cause problems down the road. The vet will also check for skin infections and sores, ear mites, intestinal worms, ticks, fleas, nutrition and general health.

Vaccinations
Don't overlook this. Vaccinations save millions of dogs' lives yearly. It is the best thing you can do to prevent such diseases as distemper, parvovirus, parainfluenza, rabies, bordetella, hepatitis and leptospirosis.

The American Veterinary Medical Association recommends that puppies receive a *series* of vaccinations, beginning at six to eight weeks of age, followed by two more vaccinations three to four weeks apart. Thereafter, renew the dog's protection with booster vaccines each year. The exception to this is the rabies boosters. The State of California requires up-to-date rabies vaccine starting at four months. Your veterinarian is the best source of advice concerning a schedule that is best for your dog.

TIP Don't take your puppy around other dogs until your veterinarian says it is okay.

Sickness & Emergencies
You should call your vet when your pet is behaving in an unusual manner which lasts. Here are a few signs to look for in a dog that signal the time to make an immediate call:
Vomiting and/or diarrhea that persists
Loss of appetite
Labored breathing
Isolation, or wanting to hide
Fever
Persistent cough
Listlessness
Increased urination or straining to urinate
Unusual odor from mouth, skin, ears or rectal area

Less Immediate signs that still need to be checked out:
A lump or bump on the skin
Lameness that persists without improvement for more than 24 hours
Persistent scratching, particularly if it results in hair loss or reddening of the skin.
Watery eyes or glassy appearance of eyes
Runny nose

Increased water intake
Weight loss

Emergency Hospitals

In an after-hour emergency call your veterinarian. If he or she is unavailable, refer to the service directory under Emergency Hospitals.

Internal Parasites

Worms can cause serious damage. Roundworm, hookworm, whipworm and tapeworm are the most common. A dog might have worms even though you don't see them in their stool. Be concerned if you notice your dog run its fanny on the floor. Your veterinarian will consider the best and safest medication for your pet.

TIP Don't give your pet medication for worms without receiving positive test results from your veterinarian.

Heartworm

These parasites are deadly. Every pet owner should be aware of this condition. Heartworm is spread by infected mosquito that bites a dog. Larvae then burrow into the dog and undergo several changes which lead to the development of worms. This large thread-like parasite lives in the right ventricle and major arteries of the heart. Ask your veterinarian to recommend a method of prevention.

External Parasites (Fleas and Ticks)

Fleas and ticks have ruined many dog-owner relationships so it's important to get a handle on this problem before it is out of control. On your initial puppy visit you should ask your veterinarian about a program and products he or she recommends. Because fleas spend most of their life off the dog, treatment of the dog is only partly effective. It is most important to eradicate fleas in the environment (indoors, outdoors, cars, etc.) and do it all at the same time.

How to Fight Fleas

Signs: *Salt and pepper-like grains about the size of sand in the coat usually around the dog's back, tail, groin and hindquarters.*

Every dog owner at one point or another will have to do battle with the dreaded flea. Adult fleas comprise only five percent of the total flea population, their eggs comprise fifty percent, larvae thirty-five percent and pupae ten percent. Fleas are most prevalent in warm weather. Fleas spend most of their life off the pet so treatment of the dog is only partly effective. To be successful you must attack not only the flea, but the flea *eggs* and the *larvae* that are in your environment. Otherwise the dog will reinfect itself when new fleas emerge.

Simultaneously mount a three-pronged attack. The main weapons are: insecticides such as *Dips*, which last about one week in Southern California, *Shampoos* especially formulated to kill adult fleas, *Powders*, which cling to a dogs coat, *Sprays*, to instantly kill adult fleas, *Bombs*, to cover large indoor areas and dog houses, *Granules*, used for the outdoor areas or on carpets to penetrate deep into the base.

Treat the dog with safe dips, shampoos. Treat inside the house with bombs, sprays, granules. Treat the yard with sprays, granules.

The Plan: Spray or use granules in the yard then treat the dogs by taking them to the groomers or give them a bath inside the home using a safe shampoo and dip (make sure the dog's eyes and ears are protected). Once the yard is safe, release the dogs in the yard and then vacuum (dispose of the bag when done), spray and bomb inside the home, or for long-term results have your house treated by an exterminator company or ask your pet supply store if they recommend a safe inorganic salt product. Don't forget to treat crates, kennel runs, bedding, garages and the car. Most insecticides will only kill adult fleas, a slow vacuum will take up eggs and larvae. To make sure, vacuum often!

TIP Buy a fine-toothed flea comb. Collect the fleas in the comb and then drown them in water laced with dish soap or flea shampoo (this can be very effective for short haired dogs).

Choose a product based on the recommendation of your veterinarian or pet store professional. Insecticides are poisons!

Pyrethrums, which are made from chrysanthemums, are claimed to be safe and effective but, like any pesticide, can be toxic if not properly used.

Use chemical flea products with caution and only as directed. Don't mix products!

Many dogs suffer allergies to flea bites called flea bite dermatitis. Some owners rub on aloe vera for relief. Consult with your veterinarian for an effective course of treatment.

Check with your veterinarian before applying an insecticide to a dog that has been wormed within a week.

Natural Flea Fighters

The following methods are natural flea treatments not scientifically proven but some owners say they work:

Avon's Skin-So-Soft diluted w/ water as a spray.
Cedar chips.
Garlic, vinegar or brewers yeast added to food.
Fine-toothed flea comb. Collect the fleas in the comb and then drown them in water laced with dish soap or flea shampoo. (This can be very effective for short haired dogs.)
Herbal flea collars.
Aloe vera drink for pets
Citrus shampoos.

Lyme Disease

Lyme disease is transmitted by the deer tick. Symptoms of the disease include fatigue, fever and swollen glands in the neck. Avoid walks in areas where deer ticks are common. Consult your veterinarian about the number of incidences in your area and check to see if he or she recommends a vaccination.

Dental Care   It is just as important for dogs to take good care of their teeth as it is for humans. Your veterinarian is also your dog's dentist. Dogs get a build up of tartar that must be removed periodically to help prevent major organ damage, tooth loss and unnecessary pain.

TIP Brush your dog's teeth regularly. Get your puppy accustomed to someone opening and examining its mouth.

10

Responsible Dog Ownership

Your Dog and Your Neighbors

All dog owners are responsible for making their dogs good neighbors. Excessive barking, unleashed roaming and unattended excretion are the major problems in urban and suburban areas. Civic leaders are banning more and more places of use for dogs because of a few irresponsible owners. Be considerate of your neighbor. If your dog barks, consider taking it inside or, for more severe problems, consult with a dog behaviorist. Always carry plastic bags on a walk. Leash your dog in public places and always practice responsible dog ownership.

Canine Good Citizenship

The AKC promotes Canine Good Citizenship with their program that encourages responsible dog ownership through training.

Your dog should be conditioned always to behave in the home, in public places, and in the presence of other dogs. The program is an evaluation that consists of ten different activities that a good canine citizen would be expected to be capable of performing. Included are such requirements as allowing a stranger to approach, walking naturally on a loose lead, walking through a crowd, sitting for examination, reacting to a strange dog and reacting to a distraction such as a door suddenly closing or a jogger running by the dog. The evaluator will inspect your dog's grooming, appearance and will evaluate your dog's performance of the sit, down and stay in position commands. The last requirement is that the dog demonstrate good manners when left alone.

General Dog Laws

Dog owners should be aware of local and state laws concerning dog ownership, some of which are described here.

Lemon Law for New Dog Owners

Retail sellers of dogs cannot sell very sick or defective dogs. Certain non-disabling problems can be disclosed and the dog can be certified as acceptable for sale by a veterinarian. If you are sold a sick or defective dog, first contact the place where you obtained the dog and seek an amicable solution to the situation. If the seller is unwilling to rectify the problem, you may be able to exercise rights under the Dog Lemon Law.

License Required

All dog owners shall apply for and obtain a separate dog license for each dog they own after it is four months old. All dog owners must possess a license at the time the dog is four months of age or thirty days after obtaining or bringing any dog four months of age into the area in which the Department of Animal Control provides licensing or animal control services. Dog owners need to renew the dog license *before* it becomes delinquent.

Restraint of Dogs by Owner

Dog owners shall at all times prevent their dogs from being at large and from being in violation of any other animal-related municipal code.

Conditions of Animal Ownership

Animal premises shall be kept sanitary and shall not constitute a fly breeding reservoir, a source of offensive odors or human or animal disease.

Public Protection from Dogs

Dog owners shall at all times prevent their dogs from biting or harassing any person engaged in a lawful act and from interfering with the lawful use of public or private property. Any person who violates any provision of this section is guilty of a misdemeanor.

Committing Nuisance

No person shall allow a dog in his/her custody to defecate or to urinate on property other than that of the owner or person having control of the dog. The failure to curb such dog and to immediately remove any feces to a proper receptacle constitutes a violation of this section. Unsighted persons relying on a guide dog shall be exempt from this section.

Female Dogs in Season

Dog owners shall securely confine their female dogs while in season within an enclosure in a manner that will prevent the attraction of male dogs in the immediate vicinity.

Disturbing the Peace Prohibited

No person shall own or harbor an animal in such a manner that the peace or quiet of the public is unreasonably disturbed. Any person who violates any provision of this section is guilty of a misdemeanor.

Inhumane Treatment and Abandonment

No person shall treat an animal in a cruel or inhumane manner or willingly or negligently cause or permit any animal to suffer unnecessary torture or pain. No person shall abandon any domestic animal without care on any public or private property. Any person who violates any provision of this section is guilty of a misdemeanor.

Transportation of Animals

No person shall transport or carry, on any public highway or public roadway, any animal in a motor vehicle not protected by a device that will prevent the animal from falling to the highway.

Animals in Unattended Vehicles

No person shall leave an animal in any unattended vehicle without adequate ventilation or in such a manner as to subject the animal to extreme temperatures which adversely affect the animal's health or welfare.

Dog Bites

Most laws state that dog owners are responsible for any dog bite injuries caused by the dog whether or not the dog was at fault. Consult your attorney for exact local and state statutes. Authorities may impound your dog for quarantine, or, if your rabies vaccine and license is up-to-date, the quarantine may be at your home. "If you are sued, the damages to the injured party may be increased if you are found to have harbored a vicious dog," according to Michael Rotsten, an Encino attorney who specializes in animal rights law.

Liability Insurance

In most states, dog owners are financially liable for any personal injury or property damage their pet causes. Someone else may be responsible if: the dog owner is less than 18 or someone other than the owner was taking care of the dog. Dog owners may be responsible for medical bills, time off work, pain and suffering, property damage, and, if the owner is found to be careless, double or triple damages or punitive damages could be declared. Consult your insurance agent to see if you are adequately covered against any risks and your local government for the laws in your area.

11

Lost & Found

**Ten Things To
Do If Your Dog
Is Lost**

The speed and thoroughness with which you react can make the difference in whether you recover your pet.

1. Organize a search party — call your friends and relatives and direct a search by foot or by car as soon as possible.

2. Ask mail carriers, paperboys, utility workers, delivery people, etc., if they have seen a stray dog. Tell a patrolling policeman.

3. Make up a card or flyer with a picture of your dog, description of your dog, your name and telephone number where you can be reached in case they spot your pet.

4. Distribute flyers to homes or mail boxes in the area you lost your dog.

5. Check all local shelters. Go in person. Don't rely on office staff to properly identify your dog over the phone. Enter your pet's information in the "lost" log and review the "found" log. Dogs without ID are held a minimum of 3 days.

6 Offer a reward, especially to neighborhood kids on bikes or skateboards.

7. Check with local veterinarians, pet shops and groomers — give them a flyer.

8. Advertise in all local newspapers. Watch the "found" ads — respond to any that might possibly be your dog.

9. Put up signs at intersections, in shopping centers, laundromats, in vet offices, pet stores and grooming parlors. Make up flyers that include a picture of your pet and both your home and work telephone numbers.

10. Don't Give Up. Often well meaning people keep a stray in their home for weeks in hopes of finding the owner.

TIP It is important that you physically go to the shelter to see if your dog is there.

Unclaimed Pets State law mandates a 72 hour hold on strays. Policy varies from shelter to shelter but usually dogs that have identification are usually kept five days while officers try to make contact with owners. After that, unclaimed pets are evaluated to determine physical condition and overall adoptability. Based on the evaluation animals are either placed up for adoption or killed by injection method. The length of time most shelters hold strays depends on their capacity at the time. Because there is a lack of space, many healthy, good tempered, highly adoptable animals are killed.

Found Pets Ask around the neighborhood. The pet may live close to you. Ask children.

Call animal control, or take the pet to the shelter yourself. That's where the owner will be looking. Use the "Found" log. Notify all shelters within a ten mile radius. Don't wait too long—some owners lose heart after a week of looking.

You could also place an advertisement in the "found" section of the newspaper (some papers do not charge), put up signs in your neighborhood and at intersections.

Call local veterinarians and groomers.

12

Travel

Airline Travel

Some airlines allow pets to be transported in the passenger cabin if the pet is in an approved carrier and can fit under the seat. Other, larger pets are placed in a pressurized compartment in the underbelly of the plane. Contact the cargo department of your airlines to receive specific information, especially if you are planning a foreign trip where quarantine time and medical certification is necessary.

TIPS You must make reservations *well in advance* preferably on a non-stop early morning flight.

Obtain an airline-approved crate in advance of your flight date. (Don't rely on the airlines.) Some airlines require a health certificate that is signed by your vet no later than 10 days prior to flight. Check with your airline. Prepare the crate. On the outside tape a piece of paper covered in plastic with your name, address, telephone numbers for both arriving and departing points, your dog's call name, the flight number, destination, and state on the paper if you are on board. Do not feed your adult pet for twelve hours before the flight, puppies sooner; allow water up until the time you leave for the airport. Check liability limitations from the airlines. Seek veterinary advice if you are considering tranquilization.

Note: In summer if the temperature is 85 degrees or higher at departure or arrival times airlines by law cannot transport your pet.

TIP Line the bottom of the carrier with a thick layer of newspaper. This will absorb any moisture and insulate against cold temperatures.

Help your dog become accustomed to the crate well in advance of the flight.

Car Travel & Vacations

Give your pet about one hour to digest a meal, Make a stop about every two to three hours for exercise, have a drink, and for relief.

Put a leash on your dog before you open the door to exit. Consider a collapsible wire crate. They are safe for motor travel and a nice place for your pet to relax.

TIP Dogs could get eye infections or injury from hanging their head out the car window.

Give your dog a chance to urinate or defecate before the trip.

Use a crate or seat harness for safety.

Choosing A Boarding Kennel

If you decide you absolutely cannot take your dog with you, then you must choose between a kennel and a dog sitter. You must use care in choosing.

To get into a good kennel, it will be necessary to make advanced reservations, especially during the summer months and around the holidays.

Visit the kennel. Ask the following questions: How big are the cages? How many dogs occupy each cage? Will they allow a special reminder of home like a favorite blanket or toy in the cage? Do they have runs so your dog does not have to be in the kennel all day? Is there shading? What about safety procedures like fire alarms, smoke detectors, and overhead sprinklers? Ask how long they have been in business and how many dogs they board. Make sure the place is well staffed during off hours. Ask if they groom at the facility or do they transport to another location. (There could be a risk of the dogs getting loose if transported.) Ask about veterinary facilities and payment in the event of medical emergency or make arrangements with your vet. Ask for a written confirmation of prices quoted and any "extras." Is the kennel clean? Is it air conditioned in the summer months? Ask about the food they provide or if you have to bring your own.

A good kennel will request proof of current vaccinations. They are required by law. You may be required to sign a release of liability. The kennel operator should be interested in your dog. Inquiries about the dog's medical history, needs, routines, food and nicknames are positive signs that your dog should receive good care. You may feel better if the kennel belongs to the American Boarding Kennel Association. This association inspects kennels, has education programs and requires members to pledge a code of ethics.

Note: Vaccines are required for boarding dogs in California. Bordetella (every 6 mo.), DHLP-CV (every year) and Rabies (every 3 years in adult dogs) are the current requirements. Check with your kennel and your veterinarian.

Ten Items for the Canine Travel Kit

1 Collar and leash.
2 ID tags with home and vacation addresses to be attached to collar.
3 Dog food and water bowls.
4 Its blanket and a couple of towels.
5 A bottle of water and a supply of food.
6 Health records & license (if required).
7 A first-aid kit with medication for motion sickness and diarrhea, etc.
8 Bedding and grooming aids.
9 Scooper, plastic bags and paper towels.
10 Favorite toy.

13

Activities & Sporting Groups

Running

Dogs need regular exercise. A big benefit of owning a dog is that a dog encourages walks and or runs that are good for both owner and dog. Before you begin running with your dog consider his breed, age and health condition. Make sure your dog is safe and on leash. Start slowly and protect your dog's feet. Be aware of extreme weather conditions. Make sure you provide plenty of water after the run, watch for injury and make sure you take plastic bags to clean up any droppings.

Dogs on the Beach

Northern California dogs are allowed <u>off-leash</u> at the following beaches:

San Luis Obispo County

Olde Port Beach

Monterey County

Carmel City Beach

Santa Cruz County

West Lighthouse Beach 6am-9am 5/1 to 9/30
Mitchell's Cove

San Francisco County

Ocean Beach
Lake Merced
Fort Funston
Crissy Field
Baker Beach

Marin County

Rodeo Beach and Lagoon
Bolinas Beach
Kehoe Beach

Dogs in the Park

Most parks require a dog to be on a leash. A few progressive communities have created special parks where dogs can enjoy a good off-leash run. They are:

Golden Gate Park Dog Run	San Francisco
Alta Plaza Park	San Francisco
Bernal Heights Park	San Francisco
Foster City Dog Exercise Area	Foster City
Boothbay Park	Foster City
San Bruno Dog Exercise Area	San Bruno
Heather Park	San Carlos
Mitchell Park	Palo Alto
Greer Park	Palo Alto
Las Palmas Park	Sunnyvale
The Dog Park	Santa Clara
Lodato Park	Scotts Valley
Garland Ranch Reg Park	Carmel Valley
Remington Dog Park	Sausalito
Marin Headlands Trail	Sausalito
Cascade Canyon	Fairfax
Memorial Park	San Anselmo
Piper Park	Larkspur
Bayfront Park (Near estuary)	Mill Valley
Ohlone Dog Park (1st dog park)	Berkeley
Claremont Canyon	Berkeley
Redwood Regional Park*	Oakland
Dracena Park	Piedmont
Pleasanton Ridge*	Pleasanton
Anthony Chabot*	Castro Valley
Alameda Creek*	Fremont
Livermore Canine Park	Livermore
Pioneer Park	Davis
Slide Hill Park	Davis
Sycamore Park	Davis
Grizzly Island Wildlife Park	Suisun
Black Diamond Mines	Antioch
Morgan Territoty Reg Preserve	Clayton
Lime Ridge Rec Area*	Concord
Las Trampas Reg Wilderness*	Danville

86

Sobrante Ridge Reg Preserve* El Sobrante
Briones Regional Park* Lafayette
Robert Sibley* Orinda
Carquinez Strait Reg Shoreline* Port Costa
Shell Ridge* Walnut Creek
Acalanes Ridge* Walnut Creek

*Leashed everywhere except developed areas (parking lots or picnic grounds).

Hiking with Your Dog

When you want to enjoy the great outdoors with your dog follow these tips:

Make sure your dog is up to date on its vaccinations (Lymes, Heartworm, etc.) and is in good health. Consult with your vet.

Train your dog with walks that increase in distance and ultimately equal the length of the planned hike.

Check in advance to see if dogs are allowed on the trail. Some parks ban dogs, others require leashed dogs, and others will allow dogs to be off leash.

Bring doggie snacks

Consider a dog pack but remember your dog is not a pack mule.

Use a leash, preferably a retractable one. Dogs that are off leash can spot a wild animal and be gone in a split second, especially the hunting breeds. Unleashed dogs can also damage sensitive plant life.

Make sure your dog has ID tags and they are securely fastened before you leave for your hike.

Bring plenty of water and a plastic bowl and don't let your pet drink stagnant water. They are susceptible to the same diseases, like giardia, that we are.

Watch out for rushing water — make sure your dog is leashed when crossing streams.

Don't let your dog approach other hikers unless the other hikers initiate the approach.

Don't forget a first aid kit that includes gauze pads, gauze, adhesive tape, disinfectant (a snake-bite kit if your area is known for snakes is a good idea) and tweezers.

Check your dog for ticks and remove immediately (make sure you get the head).

Make sure your dog does not overheat. Try to stop and rest in a shady area, if you see your dog excessively panting. Cool by giving water both internally and externally.

Consider apparel that glows in the dark or can be easily identified by hunters like a bright orange vest.

American Kennel Club (AKC)

The AKC is a club of clubs, founded by 462 show-giving clubs to help organize the sport. The AKC is "dedicated to advancing the study, breeding, exhibiting, running and maintenance of thoroughbred dogs." There are 145 breeds and over 1.2 million purebred dogs registered every year.

The AKC licenses dog shows, field trials, obedience trials, tracking tests, hunting and lure coursing tests, herding tests and trials, and coonhound hunts. It maintains the official record of these events and also maintains various systems of administrative review.

To enter a show or obtain show date information see Superindendents in Service Directory.

Dog Shows

Dog shows are evaluations of a dog's conformation. Most dogs seen at shows are competing for points toward their championship.

After examination of the entry, each judge decides how close the dog measures up, in his or her opinion, to the official *breed standard.* The dogs are compared against each other and placed from first to fourth. It takes fifteen points to become a champion of record and use the "CH" Title. The number of points awarded are based on the number of dogs at the show, the more dogs, the more points. Also, the points are adjusted depending on breed, the sex and the geographical location of the show. A dog can earn from one to five points at a show. Wins of three, four or five points are considered "majors." The fifteen points required for championship must be won under at least three different judges, and must include two majors won under different judges.

Obedience Trials

Obedience Trials test a dog's ability to perform a prescribed set of exercises.

A judge scores three different levels, with each level being more difficult. AKC awards titles for successful completion of Novice (CD), Open (CDX) and the third, and most difficult, Utility (UD). A competitor who gets more than 50% of the points on each exercise and a total score of 170 or more out of a possible 200 earns a "leg" towards an obedience degree or title. Three legs are required for a degree. The ultimate distinction, for those dogs that have earned their utility titles, is an Obedience Trial Champion (OTCH) title.

Junior Showmanship

This is an entire class of AKC competition for youngsters between the ages of 10 and 18 that helps them develop handling skills. This class of competition is judged solely on the ability and skills of the handler.

Title	CD	Companion Dog
Terminology	CDX	Companion Dog Excellent
	CG	Certificate of Gameness
	UD	Utility Dog
	OTCh	Obedience Trial Champion
	Ch	Champion
	FCh	Field Champion
	HCH	Herding Championship
	HI	Herding Intermediate
	HIC	Herding Instinct Certificate
	HS	Herding Started
	HX	Herding Excellent
	JH	Junior Hunter
	LCM	Lure Courser of Merit
	ROM	Register of Merit
	SH	Senior Hunter
	TD	Tracking Dog
	TDX	Tracking Dog Excellent
	TT	Temperament Tested
	WC	Working Certificate
	WCX	Working Certificate Excellent
	WDX	Working Dog Excellent

Triple Champion, title awarded to a dog that has won show, obedience and trial championships.

Professional Handlers

Anyone aspiring to have a career as a professional dog handler or anyone requiring the services of a professional dog handler may write or call:

Professional Handlers Association
Kathleen Bowser, Secretary (No Joke)
15810 Mount Everest Lane
Silver Springs, MD 20906
301 924-0089

Herding Dogs

In the testing section, dogs can earn titles of Herding Test Dog (HT) and Pre-Trial Tested Dog (PT).

AKC trials offer four titles, beginning with the Herding Started (HS), Herding Intermediate (HI), and Herding Excellent (HX). After earning an HX, dogs can then accumulate the necessary fifteen championship points for the Herding Championship (HCH).

Den Trials

Group of hunt instinct tests for breeds bred to hunt underground. Open to all Terrier breeds and Dachshunds that can fit into a 9" square tunnel. Dogs stalk rats through tunnels ranging 10 to 30 feet. (This is a bloodless sport.)

Agility Training

Agility is a lot of fun. This sport is like a visit to a doggy amusement park that provides an outlet for energy and a great way to spend some free time with your companion.

In this sport dogs traverse a maze of obstacles and compete for speed and accuracy. Dogs jump through tires, zip through tunnels, scale a 6-foot-tall A-frame, walk a narrow "dog walk," negotiate a see-saw, zig-zag through poles and soar over a variety of hurdles. Dogs can participate early. They learn to improve their skill with practice.

Carting Equipment

Summerfield Specialties
PO Box 2346
Spring Valley, CA 91979
619 461-7324
Cart & Harness

Field Trial and Hunting Clubs

Field trials are held separately for Pointing breeds, Retrievers and Spaniels, as well as Beagles, Basset Hounds and Dachshunds. Field trials are practical demonstrations of the dog's ability to perform in the field, the function for which they were bred. AKC titles that are awarded are Field Champion and Amateur Field Champion.

Hunting tests are for retrievers, pointing breeds and Spaniels. AKC evaluates the dog's performance on three levels, with each level increasing in difficulty. The levels are Junior (JH), Senior (SH) and Master Hunter (MH). Dogs are judged on their hunting, bird finding, marking, retrieving and trained ability.

Tracking Tests

Tracking tests the dog's ability to follow a scent. A dog that passes this test earns a AKC Tracking Dog title (TD). Advanced work can earn a Tracking Dog Excellent (TDX) title.

Flyball

This is a great team sport that requires your dog to jump over four small obstacles and retrieve a tennis ball by thumping a container that is set to spring-out the ball and return with the ball to the start area. The next team member then starts, and so on, until all team members have finished. You are racing against another team and the team that finishes first wins.

Scent Hurdle Racing

Dogs run over the same hurdles as flyball, but they must pick out their owners' dumbell by scent from a set of four and return. Also run as a relay. Check with your local obedience club.

Lure Coursing

Dogs chase a simulated game over an open course of some 550 to 1800 yards that tests speed and agility. Breeds allowed to run by the American Sighthound Field Association are: Afghans, Basenjis, Borzois, Greyhounds, Ibizans, Irish Wolfhounds, Pharaoh Hounds, Salukis, Scottish Deerhounds and Whippets, all of which follow their quarry by sight. The purpose is "to preserve and further develop the natural beauty, grace, speed, and coursing skill of the sighthound." The association accepts only registered dogs from AKC, UKC, National Greyhound Assoc., or must possess a critic number from the Saluki Club of America.

Schutzhund

This rigorous German sport combines tracking, obedience and protection exercises. While dogs of other breeds are admitted, this sport is primarily for the German Shepherd Dog. Schutzhund, meaning "protection dog," measures endurance, ability to scent, courage, mental stability and trainability. The sport recognizes both the handler's ability to train and the dog's ability to perform. Choose your trainer with great care.

Appendix A
Local Breeders and Breed Club Directory

Northern California Breeders Directory

The following list of breeders is offered as an aid to the public in obtaining purebred dogs. Breeders listed were obtained from AKC show guides, national and local breed clubs and word of mouth. *Northern California Dog Owners Guide* does not recommend, guarantee, endorse, nor rate breeders and kennels. Although we strive hard to include reputable breeders, we do not assume any liability. You must exercise good judgement. Read Chapter 3, what to look for from a quality breeder. Buyer beware.

Breeders — If you are a local breeder and you would like to be included in this directory, please submit a letter of application with qualifications to the publisher at the address in the front of the book. Please include references from other breeders listed or clubs. If you need to change a listing, please fill out a change form located in the back of this book.

Puppy Owners, Veterinarians or Rescuers — If you have a complaint against any breeder listed, please write a detailed letter to the publisher at the address in the front of the book.

Affenpinscher
Affenpinscher Club of America
2006 Scenic Rd Tallahassee, FL 32303 Ms. Terry Graham, Sec
Howard Dees   209 745-1224

Afghan Hounds
Afghan Hound Club of America, Inc
2408A Rt 31, Oswego, IL 60543 Ms. Norma Cozzoni, Sec
Monterey Bay Afghan Hound Club   Mike Dunham   408 663-2637
Northern California Afghan Hound Club   Mary Jean Odron   209 931-4682
Mary Jean Or Ed Odron   209 931-4682

Dog Owners Guide

Pam Or Lonnie Patterson		408 263-4698
Richard Sousa	Coastwind	408 663-2637
Vicki Or Warren Cook		408 688-7508
Bobbie Or Bob Keller		408 738-2176
Karen Or Keith Erb		408 761-3095
Cathy Lursen		408 847-2336
Susan Netboy		415 851-7812
Sandra Wornum		415 924-7020
Everett Bollen Jr	J' Belle	510 278-5874
Pat Or Gary Kunich		510 625-1775
Ine Harris		510 849-4823
Rose Upper	Talisman	707 546-5610
Gail Kramer		707 584-2942
Jean Perlstein		707 762-7626
Betsy Hufnagel	Cavu	707 894-4007
Tracy Olsen	Cabaret	707 939-9582
Alison Gray		916 967-5076
Pat Or George Patterson		916 989-0675

Airedale Terrier
Airedale Terrier Club of America
47 Tulip Ave., Ringwood, NJ 07456 Dr Suzanne Hampton, Sec

California Airedale Terrier Club	Ms Linda Hobbet	408 865-0779
Barbara Cissel	Cisseldale	209 291-0762
Patty Gregg	209 847-1633	
Marsha Sarkisian Or Linda Hobbet	Bluacre	408 865-0779
Karen Lapierre	415 493-3033	
James Brennan	Windward	415 820-1162
Ron Or Lee Colvin Norel	510 447-9237	
Liz	916 678-5040	
Pat Wormington	916 832-5235	

Akita
Akita Club of America
761 Lonesome Dove Lane Copper Canyon, TX 75067 Nancy Henry, Sec

Golden Gate Akita Club	Robert Kopico	415 355-4230
Gold Country Akita Club		916 961-8835
Dorothy Warren	Ranchlake	408 867-2467
Carol Foti	Kosetsu	415 488-0886
Marc Or Sue Manning	Mars	415 756-5590
Stephen Or Sharon Gignilliat		707 447-5893
Susan Duncan		707 448-7643
Mortishia Fairchild	Jem	707 552-3825

Alaskan Malamute
Alaskan Malamute Club of America
187 Grouse Creek Rd, Grants Pass, OR 97526 Ms Sharon Weston, Sec

Nancy Guadagria	Nabo	209 835-7445
Susie Or Al Richardson	Tanunak	209 835-8524
Bill & Debbie Griffith	Toneeka	408 365-0934
Nancy Kessler		415 282-5738

94

Wendy Corr		510 528-1529
Vickey Palmer		510 827-3378
James & Joyce Keesling	Tono	916 676-2364
Rebecca Morin		916 987-0537

American Eskimo (Standard)
American Eskimo Dogs Club of America
Rt 3 Box 211-B Stroud, OK 74079 Carolyn Jester, Sec
North American Eskimo Dog Club

Dennis Blickenstaff		408 258-8663
California American Eskimo Assoc	Lisa Castelan	805 833-6377
Shirley Tooker	Star	209 522-2717
Theresa Dreesbach		408 663-2338
Dawn Marie	Crystalfey	510 796-2333
Catherine Martoline		702 322-7544
Tammy Nichols	Krystal	702 348-7957
Darlene Poole		702 972-9161
Donna Hayes		916 649-6733

American Foxhound
American Foxhound Club
1221 Oakwood Ave Dayton, OH 45419 Mrs Jack Heck, Sec

Paul Or Karen Crary	Pacific	408 629-9269

American Pit Bull Terrier
Amreican Pit Bull Terrier Club
Rt 2 Box 1157, Denton, TX 76201

	Patty Murley	817 787-2107
Shannon Johnson	Shadytown	209 667-7839
Pam Carter	Gaffs	209 667-4210
Sharon Duvall		916 674-9447

American Staffordshire Terrier
Staffordshire Terrier Club of America
785 Valley View Rd Forney, TX 75126 H Richard Pascoe, Sec

Am Staffordshire Terrier Club of Greater LA	Breed Club	818 716-8224
Sharon Duvall		916 674-9447

American Water Spaniel
American Water Spaniel Club
2600 Grand St NE Minneapolis, MN 55418 Carolyn Kraskey, Sec

American Wirehaired Pointing Griffon
36340 Hillside Lane Lebanon, OR 97355 Kathryn Haberkorn, Sec

Anatolian Shepherd
Anatolian Shepherd Dog Club of America
PO Box 880-D Alpine, CA 91903 Quinn Harned, Sec

		619 445-3334
Windy Springs		510 634-4933
Janice Or James Frasche	Semavi	916 488-2707
Pat Dougherty	Shenandoah	916 394-8004

Dog Owners Guide

Australian Cattle Dog

Australian Cattle Dog Club of America
24605 Lewiston Blvd Hampton, MN 55031, Bellie Johnson, Sec

Marge Blankenship	Heeler Hill	707 643-6604
Liz Or Russ Evans	Austcados	707 778-6689
Daniel Or Seana Powell		916 244-7235
Barbara Peach		916 275-4910
Kathy Christian	Wagga Wagga	916 620-4159

Australian Shepherd

United States Australian Shepherd Assoc.
PO Box 4317, Irving, TX 75015, Sherry Ball, Sec
Australian Shepherd Club of America
P O Box 921 Warwick NY 10990

Shannon & Gayle Oxford		209 727-3130
Carrie Rollins & Curt Christensen		707 763-7003
Clara Brown	Windrift	707 795-5010
Mark Or Julie Brown	Autumnhill	916 894-5947
Ann Atkinson	Ebbtide	707 894-3183
Judy Boone		916 687-8727

Australian Terrier

Australian Terrier Club of America
1515 Davon Lane, Nassau Bay, TX 77058 Ms Marilyn Harban, Sec

Sandra & Craig Lassen	Blackoak	707 876-3136
Earl Or Judy May		916 742-8506
Susan Bentley	Benayr	916 795-2480

Basenji

Basenji Club of America, Inc
PO Box 1076, South Bend, IN 46624 Ms Susan Patterson-Wilson, Sec

Basenji Club of Northern Cal	Susan Fairweather	
Bob Or Nancy Brinton	Pharaon	408 262-4449
Charles Mullins Jr	Abutu	408 294-6900
Mary Ann Palm	Palm Desert	408 425-7650
Nancy Black	Kiburi	408 779-0862
Margaret Hoff	Kucha	415 453-2510
Susan Fairweather	Takabari	415 457-5261
Bobbie Or Walt Lynch	Sheshe	415 892-3248
Pat Cembura	Arubmec	510 222-3989
Sarah Weyland		510 516-1092
Eleanor Or Tobie	Kontobi	510 569-2549
Marilyn Or Ken Leighton	Zuri	510 846-5300
Pat Fragassi	Tanza	510 846-9204
Maxine Or Mel Stringer	Marabasi	707 429-4898
Sandy Perez		707 525-9307
Teri Brennan		707 552-8182
Michael Or Kathy Pine	Umbuji	916 961-8288

Appendix A: Local Breeders and Breed Club Directory

Basset Hound

Basset Hound Club of America, Inc
2343 Peters Rd Ann Arbor, MI 48103   Andrea Field, Sec
Northern California Basset Hound Club   Brian Littleton
Basset Hound Club of Sacramento   Sharron Lenth   916 791-4059
Lim & Sharon Dok   Castlehill   408 847-1360
Ruth Wilcox   510 562-8336
Jim Chester   510 828-2322
Linda Moore   Treetop   707 642-8690
Marianne Paulsson   Reepa's   707 823-4543
B Hollandsworth   Sweethome   916 343-4209

Beagle

National Beagle Club
River Rd. Bedminster NJ 07921   Joseph Wiley Jr.
Beaglers of San Joaquin   Mary Keegan   415 349-2560
Northern California Beaglers Club   Suzan Murray
Blossom Valley Beagle Club   Judy Musladin
Central California Beagle Club   Richard Jacobs   909 787-9356
Mary Powell & Trudy Rivera   408 244-1804
Paul Or Karen Crary   Pacific   408 629-9269
John & Greta Haag   Greenwood   510 549-3940
Joyce & Jeff Dayton   510 838-2878
Tracy Olsen   Cabaret   707 939-9582
Carolyn Price   Car-Don   916 824-4756
Beverly Millette   916 673-1925

Bearded Collie

Bearded Collie Club of America
1116 Carpenter's Trace, Villa Hills, KY 41017, Ms Diana Siebert, Sec
Sacramento Valley Bearded Collie Fanciers   916 457-7012
     Sinda Unicorn   916 682-6979
Mary Edner   916 988-2232
R Colavecchio   916 988-9799

Beauceron

North American Beauceron Club
106 Halteman Rd Pottstown PA 19461   S Bulanda
Beauceron Club of America
225 South St Glen Falls, NY 12801   909 767-9163

Bedlington Terrier

Bedlington Terrier Club of America
PO Box 11, Morrison, IL 61270, Mr Robert Bull, Sec
Bedlington Terrier Club of the West   Breed Club   619 576-9714
Marjorie Hanson   Valgos   619 435-7393
Robin Boyett   Mutt Hutt   619 576-9714
Chris Williams   619 747-4492

Dog Owners Guide

Belgian Malinois
American Belgian Malinois Club
1717 Deer Creek Rd Central Valley, CA 96019 Ms Barbara Peach,916 275-4910
J Robles		206 886 1316
Jean Adams		916 221-0927
Barbara Peach		916 275-4910

Belgian Sheepdog
Belgian Sheepdog Club of America, Inc
2530 Harbison Rd Cedarville, OH 45314 Mrs. Phyllis Davis, Sec
Kaye Hall		707 255-0683
Ellen Haro	Greenfield	916 678-3888

Belgian Tervuren
American Belgian Tervuren Club, Inc
4970 Chinook Trail Casper, WY 82604 Ms Nancy Carman, Sec
Ri Or Se Symons	Symons	408 779-6136
Cheryl Brandeberry	After Shock	415 341-8269
Clara Brown	Windrift	707 795-5010
Carmen Hilgesen	Snowflower	916 661-7029

Bernese Mountain Dog
Bernese Mountain Dog Club of America, Inc
812 Warren Landing Fort Collins, CO 80525 Ms Roxanne Bortnick, Sec
Carolyn Or Eric Laforge	Laforge	415 898-0625
Lynn & Joseph Wynne		510 938-5456
Marty Or Carolyn Lockhart	Car-Mar	707 545-5819
Nancy Hendricks	Windrider	707 743-2445
Maner Hite		707 778-6860
Ann Nichols	Nighttime	707 935-1174

Bichon Frises
Bichon Frises Club of America, Inc
Route 2, Gulch Lane, Twin Falls, ID 83301 Mrs Bernice Richardson, Sec
Bichon Frise Club of Northern Cal	Virginia Boswell	916 487-7143
Virginia Boswell		916 487-7143

Black & Tan Coonhound
American Black & Tan Coonhound Club, Inc
700 Grand Ave Elgin, IL 60120   Victoria Blackburn, Sec
Maner Hite		707 778-6860

Bloodhound
American Bloodhound Club
1914 Berry Lane, Daytona Beach, FL 32124 Mr Ed Kilby, Sec
Paula Pevear		916 221-0217

Bolognese
Bolognese Club of America
PO Box 1461 Montrose, CO 81402 Dorothy Goodale, Sec   303 249-6492

Appendix A: Local Breeders and Breed Club Directory

Border Collies
Border Collie Club of America
6 Pinecrest Lane, Durham, NH 03824   Janet Larson, Sec
United States Border Collie Club
Rt 1, Box 23, White Post, VA 22663
Border Collie Society of America
2514 Tregaron Ave., Louisville, KY 40299

Shannon & Gail Oxford		209 727-3130
Dan & Susan Hoag	Oak Ridge	408 484-9850
Jerry & Lynn Buck	Meadowlark	408 578-0959
Sharon Bickford		415 327-2931
Don Hanes	Karnehros	707 255-0584
Karen Kollgaard	Shoestring	707 575-3828
Mary Ann Jacobson	Tunnel Hill	707 964-5125
Russell & Darlene Drake	River Ridge	805 688-8250
Carla Poponey		916 541-2178
Edward Or Donna Seigmund		916 549-3324
Bill & Margie Scott	Quarry House	916 624-8414
Dan & Geri Byrne	In Action	916 664-5871
Tony & Lynn Diaz	Fame Farms	916 678-9022
Lin Daugherty		916 742-8695
Tom & Patti Duffy	Back 40	916 743-4772
Robert & Broa Mcgrew	Mcgrew	916 758-4176

Border Terrier
Border Terrier Club of America,Inc
832 Lincoln Blvd Manitowoc, WI 54220 Mrs Laurale Stern, Sec

Border Terrier Club of the Redwoods	Mary Ainsworth	510 537-8704
Cathy Kaiser	Jericho	707 995-0531
Linda		916 286-3807

Borzoi
Borzoi Club of America, Inc
29 Crown Dr Warren, NJ 07059   Mrs Karen Mays, Sec

Borzoi Club of Northern California	Suzan Mallone	510 679-9818
Lynn Green		209 245-6088
Sandy Holley	Shady Luck	209 526-0205
Fern Lockrem		510 625-4044
Susan Mallone		510 679-9818
Tracy Olsen	Cabaret	707 939-9582

Boston Terrier
Boston Terrier Club of America, Inc
8537 East San Burno Dr Scottsdale, AZ 85258 Ms Marian Sheehan, Sec

Golden Gate Boston Terrier Club	Carol Enright	916 486-3647
Patricia Stone		408 371-7452
Joan Howard		415 672-8564
Victoria Cochran	Luckylady	510 284-1882
Susan Malione		510 679-9818
Lynda Piercy	Wannabe Run	916 343-5171
Sheri Lattus	Blossom Run	916 345-1220
Lois Fraser Fraser	River City	916 363-1789

Jeanette Mellen		916 679-2113
Allison Davis	Berryesa	916 895-8062
Mary & Norman Anderson	Andi	916 961-8343

Bouvier des Flandres

American Bouvier des Flanders Club, Inc
Rt 1 Box 201, Delaplane, VA 22025   Ms Diane Ring, Sec

Sue Gigiorno	Susants	916 933-0142
Cindy Strumm		707 963-5774

Boxer

American Boxer Club, Inc
6310 Edward Dr Clinton, MD 20735 Mrs Barbara Wagner, Sec

Golden Gate Boxer Club	Virginia Bradley	408 722-5862
East Bay Boxer Club	Dorthy Hart	707 253-8897
Sacramento Valley Boxer Club	Alma Pomeroy	916 622-8584
Lynda Yon		209 832-2897
Paula Johnson		510 484-4075
Ken Morrison	Bay View	510 799-4618
David Schroeder		707 449-1728
Wendy Morawski	Skidoo's	707 644-7327
Brian Thompson		707 778-8002
Glenn Or Zona Grupe	Glenroe	707 864-1814
Dr Paul & Sue Gepard		916 489-9387
Alaina & Bob Pomaroy		916 622-8584
Sally Filice		916 642-2697
Paula Duncan		916 672-0326

Briard

Briard Club of America, Inc
547 Sussex Ct Elk Grove Village, IL 60007 Ms Janet Wall, Sec

Chuck Christianson		707 869-9090
Denis Or Marsha Gough	Nuage Noir	916 533-5079
Robert & Mary Lopez		916 633-4929
Donavan Thompson		916 923-2253

Brittany

American Brittany Club, Inc
800 Hillmont Ranch Rd Aledo, TX 76008Ms Joy Searcy, Sec

Northern California Brittany Club	Helen Brown	
Golden Empire Brittany Club	Beverly Millette	916 673-1925
Sherry Or Bud Larsen	Almaden	209 323-8978
Pennie Peterson	Shiloh's Blazen	408 683-4878
Fred Kewell		415 833-8349
Jessica Or Rhonda Alar		510 582-2714
Ned Castillo	Castles	510 938-0638
Arlene Mccabe Or Michelle Chaney	Mich's	707 252-2125
Laura Barsuglia		707 523-1389
Carol Or Irvin Harris	Starline	707 552-5816
Beverly Millette		916 673-1925

Appendix A: Local Breeders and Breed Club Directory

Brussels Griffon
American Brussels Griffon Association
Box 56 221 E Scott Grand Ledge, MI 48837 Mr Terry Smith, Sec

Joan Guest	Selfon	415 375-8393
Pat Hamann	Rickshaw	510 234-4146
Barbara Yamasaki		510 758-4565

Bull Terrier
Bull Terrier Club of America

10477 Ethel Cr Cypress, CA 90630	Susan Murphy, Sec	
Barbary Coast Bull Terrier Club	Nan Stodder	
Michael & Nancy May		707 545-8101
Robert Or Bonnie Erwin	Pippen Hill	707 823-9085
Esther Abshier	Two Step	916 895-0321

Bulldog
Bulldog Club of America

8810 M Street, Omaha, NE 68127,	Ms Linda Sims, Sec	
Bulldog Club of Northern California	Maxine Murdoch	408 726-2723
Mother Lode Bulldog Club of Sacramento	Claudia Marcus	916 989-3963
Maxine Murdock	Murdock	408 623-9055
Mary Aiken	Silverspoon	415 344-0273
Lillian Davis	Terra Nova	415 355-0399
Paula Braz	Shabrae	510 686-1881
Don Or Barbara Dell	Delitebull	707 525-9561
Floyd Thompson		707 795-6169
Sandy Barron		916 725-6526
Matt Boyd Boyds		916 737-7609

Bullmastiff
American Bullmastiff Association, Inc
Box 137D Burger Rd Melbourne, KY 41059 Ms Mary Anne Duchin, Sec

Patricia O'Brien	Bullmast	310 421-9354
Stanley & Jill Cohen	Sea Star	310 457-9684
Taun Brooks	Wild Heart	619 369-2400
Stan & Claudia Stankiewicz		619 575-0541
Terry Gaskins	Upper Crust	619 697-7075
Darrell & Evie Johnson		619 789-7425
Carol Beans	Tauralan	714 544-1824
Pat O'Brien	Bullmast	714 870-5235
Carol Haddon	Von Haddon	805 466-9312

Cairn Terrier
Cairn Terrier Club of America
8096 Chilson Rd Pinckney, MI 48169Christine Bowlus, Sec

Cairn Terrier Club Of Northern California	Ruth Barstow	415 472-3509
Cairn Terrier Club Of Northern California		415 388-6708
Cairn Terrier Club Of Northern California	Clare Hanna	510 522-5892
Barbara Walker	Cairnbawn	415 388-6708
Ruth Barstow		415 472-3509
Jeff Greer	Fiddler Green	415 892-9632

Gloria Kregoski		916 622-5156
Jim Roswurm		916 677-8898

Canaan Dog
Canaan Dog Club of America

3707 Falcon Way, Egen, MN 55123	Marjie Weinberger	612 688-8811
Joan Capaio		916 687-7663

Cane Corso
International Cane Corso Federation
PO Box 212 Hainesport, NJ 08036 609 265-0029

Catahoulas, Louisiana
National Association of Louisiana Catahoulas

PO Box 1040 Denham Springs, LA 70727		504 665-6082
Mary McInnes	Golden State	909 823-8279

Cavalier King Charles Spaniel
Cavalier King Charles Spaniel Club

434 Country Lane Louisville KY 40207	Suzanne Brown	502 897 9148
Joanne & James Nash	Rambler	415 964-0181
Marilyn Hill	Hillhaven	510 799-2682

Cesky Terrier
The National Cesky Terrier Club
PO Box 445, Rockway, NJ 07866
The Cesky Terrier Club of America

PO Box 1318 Col Falls. MT 59912		406 892-5079

Chesapeake Bay Retriever
American Chesapeake Club, Inc

1705 Rd 76 Pasco, WA 99301	Ms Janel Hopp	
Sylvia Holderman	Meadowood	408 426-6964
Adey May Dunnell		707 425-3766
Lisa Van Loo	Farallon	707 448-8087
Kathy Miller	Sandy Oak	707 823-3148
Kellie Lewis		916 620-6030
Les Or Nancy Lowenthal	Berteleda	415 388-2173
Elizabeth Reed		916 529-0910

Chihuahua
Chihuahua Club of America, Inc

5019 Village Trail San Antonio, TX 78218 Ms Lynnie Bunten, Sec		
Chihuahua Club of Northern California	Flo Bell	707 525-9575
Virginia Smith	Ginjim	209 266-4427
Barbara Davis		209 299-1609
Pat Porreca		209 836-9021
Sharon Hermosilo		408 279-4444
Karen Abe		415 728-5015
Delores Chambers	Fantasia	510 687-2888
Jill Or Bill Green		510 827-1880
Shirley Emmons	Dee Po	707 224-4192
Bonnie Or Cathy	Whitecliff	707 426-6254
Roberta Woodward	Dejavu	707 525-9575

Appendix A: Local Breeders and Breed Club Directory

Flo Bell	Beldevus	707 525-9575
Rose Upper	Talisman	707 546-5610
Elaine Pardee	Pixie	707 538-3655
Famous Or Margie Holt	Dreamweaver	707 792-2395
Dottie Boyza		916 223-5463
Judy		916 991-0127

Chinese Crested Dog

American Chinese Crested Club
3101 E Blount St Pensacola, FL 32503   Ms Lynda Nagel

Charles Fugita	510 233-8553
Lou Ells	916 743-8028
Jani Johnson	916 371-2720

Chow Chow

Chow Chow Club, Inc
3580 Plover Place Seaford, NY 11783   Irene Cartabio, Sec
Redwood Coast Chow Chow Club   Candy Ishmael   707 578-4703

	Lewis Cuccia	510 233-4500
Holley Mckay		209 924-3323
Joyce Balbontin		415 967-3099
Lewis Or Nancy Cuccia		510 233-4500
Bruce Shayne		510 426-1161
Charles Wiseman		510 439-8838
Fred Or Brenda Buechler	Rhapsody	510 672-0427
Fran Or Pete Martinez		510 783-8045
Brenda Driessan	Sanders	707 428-3638
Joanna Bushby		707 462-9251
Eugene Or Eileen Baldi		707 539-6234
Kerry Or Candy Ishmael		707 578-4703
Prudence Baxter	Tamarin	707 664-9248
Sue Estrada		916 427-0145
Tom Torres Or Rubin Rios		916 532-9224
Ray Cadena		916 661-3444
William Or Barbara Cervan		916 722-8040
Charles Or Stacy Kruse		916 723-6649
Joe Or Arlene Solis		916 791-2826
Pauline Or Harry Proveaux		916 863-0335
Kaye Cooper Ballard		916 965-1261

Clumber Spaniel

Clumber Spaniel Club of America
9 Cedar Street Selden, NY 11784 Ms Barbara Stebbins, Sec

Paula Or Marla		415 589-3168
Flo Bell	Beldevus	707 525 9575
Jean Adams		916 221-0927

Cocker Spaniel

American Spaniel Club, Inc
845 Old Stevens Creek Rd Martinez, GA 30907 Margaret Ciezkowski

Mission Valley Cocker Spaniel Club	Leslie Puppo	707 446-8581
Bay Cities Cocker Spaniel Club	Barbara Peterson	510 228-4720
San Joaquin Valley Cocker Spaniel Club	Della Rush	209 255-3266
Elaine Dal Bon		415 892-5469
Anita Roberts	Memoir	415 897-8747
Vera Sell	Verandah	510 439-8335
Robert & Sally Clenner	Top-C	510 634-8672
Beverly Marsh	Summer Dream	707 224-0916
Sandy Bailey	That's It	707 447-8737
Janet Little	Mistiwind	707 544-1009
Cheryl Or Ralph Germani		707 763-0125
Lorraine Carver	Sete Mares	707 763-3477
Rose Mary Smalley	T Rose	707 987-9734
Angie Or Cliff	Holloway	916 741-0211
Amy Weiss		916 988-1817
Romona Miller	Seenar	916 991-6755

Collie

Collie Club of America, Inc
1119 South Fleming Rd Woodstock, IL 60098 Mrs Carmen Leonard, Sec

Collie Club of Northern California	Janet Chavez	408 729-6689
California Collie Fanciers	Dianne Parness	
Sacramento Valley Collie Club	JoAnne Hawkins	707 995-9244
Bob Or Roz Durham		916 865-3091
Jean Roberts	Windsong	707 252-2134
Diana Mclaughlin	Applewood	707 823-0472

Collie, Smooth

American Smooth Collie Assoc.

1368 Valley View Rd. Ashland OR 97520	Jan Anders	503 482 1435
Jackie & Dick Potter		510 930-7210

Corgi, Cardigan Welsh

Cardigan Welsh Corgi Club of America,Inc
PO Box 141 Moody, AL 35004 Dr Kathleen Harper, Sec

Dennis Or Patricia Seifert	707 449-3967
George Or Marge Sparks	916 549-5219

Corgi, Pembroke Welsh

Pembroke Welsh Corgi Club of America, Inc
2601 Bancroft Lane Louisville, KY 40241 Mr John Vahaly

G G Pembroke Welsh Corgi Fanciers	Joan Jensen	415 474-4498
Carol Barlick	Carolee	408 252-3259
Lee Bear	Bear Acre	408 268-0365
Sally Howe	Howbout	408 378-7346
Susan Stanley	Pempono	408 867-6897
Barbara Mathiesen	Green Oaks	415 375-1991
Joan & Raymond Jensen	Martindale	415 474-4498
William Lloyd	Willoyd	415 837-9382

Appendix A: Local Breeders and Breed Club Directory

Thomas Mathiesen	Nebriowa	415 851-2702
Lois Riesenberg		510 254-3254
Vera Sell	Verandah's	510 439-8335
Pat Pettipeice	Pettiwood	510 634-4699
Margaret Downing	Cappykor	510 685-3685
James Warburton	Denbigfox	510 933-3648
Ida Anderson	Hedgeside	707 224-6886
Jan Sheets	Cypress	707 449-4776
Kay Hammel	Tams	707 792-2859
Sharon Curry	Shonleh	707 823-2342
Romona Sergent	Seren	707 823-1804
Harriett Campbell		707 935-6701
Pat Jensen	Larchmont	707 996-0356
Sheridan Lattus	Blossom Run	916 345-1220
Janice Edwards	Penway	916 381-0378
Debra Gibson		916 687-7275
Gibson Reid	Jade Tree	916 689-1661
Michael Stone		916 742-1617
Terry Hansen	Pinemead	916 743-7753
Judith Or Dawn Vargas	Linvar	916 791-7423
Katherine Runkle	Caleb	916 972-8521
Lonette Crider	Fox-Cri	916 991-2003

Curly-Coated Retriever

Curly-Coated Retriever Club of America
24 Holmes Blvd Ft Walton Beach, FL 32548 Gina Columbo

Leslie Puppo	Avanti	707 446-8581
Kimberly Kieran		707 664-1708

Dachshund

Dachshund Club of America, Inc
390 Eminence Pike Shelbyville, KY 40065 Mr Walter Jones, Sec

East Bay Dachshund Club	Mary B Cushman	510 837-4005
Northern California Dachshund Club	Diane Heldebrant	916 485-5950
Golden Gate Dachshund Club	Arthur Sanderson	
Jody Irolla		209 225-5639
Sue Mcclelland	Sioux	209 579-3185
Brad Or Patty Mcdonald		209 673-3112
Don Smith	Rodon	209 838-6559
Karin Or Kyle Covell		408 268-0672
Elbert Or Elizabeth Benjamin	Bedoxeld	510 223-1581
Sharon Taylor (Miniatures)	Heinder	707 447-9513
Flo Bell	Beldevus	707 525-9575
Art Grundish Or Kim Wetch	Rosadach's	707 585-9222
Diane Or Gordon	Hildebrant	916 485-5950
Claire Mcphail		916 784-4000
Greta Roberts (Mini)	Deanza	408 247-3789
Sharon Or Robert Jadick (Mini)	Tinytales	510 682-7844
Susan Kramer (Mini)	Dakalhunds	916 726-0907
Dayrl Or Art Sandar (Mini)		916 877-6010
Sue Mccelland (Wire)	Sioux's Zoo	209 527-5177
Scott Or Beverly Brennesholtz	Khybren	916 671-4514
Art Or Daryl		916 877-6010

Romona Miller   Seenar   916 991-6755
Roberta Woodward (Long Coat)   Dejavu   707 525-9575
Kate Whitney (Wire)   Neydachs   916 342-2009

Dalmatian

Dalmatian Club of America, Inc
4390 Chickasaw Rd Memphis, TN 38117 Mrs Anne Fleming, Sec

Dalmation Club of Northern California	Joanne Nash	415 964-0181
Stephen Or Karen Rochin	Sunrunner	408 629-7430
Michael Heflin		510 893-0538
Denise Powell		707 525-8842
James Or Suzette Cahill	Knottingham	707 526-0507
Marti Nickoli	Nickoli	707 526-7542
Camilla Gray	Dairydell	707 762-6111
Elizabeth Johnson	Feather River	916 534-3250
Fred Or Myrtle Klensch	Pacificia	916 652-6998
David & Bonnie Miller		916 761-6924
Hal & Cathy Shore		916 962-0722

Dandie Dinmont

Dandie Dinmont Terrier Club of America, Inc
25 Ridgeview Rd Staunton, VA 24401 Mrs Mixon Darracott, Sec

Roy Or Betty Ann Stenmark		415 851-8190
Max & Linda Spurlock		510 524-7123
Christy Maxfield	Chrisfield	510 797-9694
Nancy Herman	Mackilty	510 846-9520
Janet Little	Mistiwind	707 544-1009
Edward Murry Or Chris Sloan	Kemp	707 869-3160
Dora Ortwein	Kamlo	707 996-9472

Doberman Pinscher

Doberman Pinscher Club of America
10316 NE 136th Pl Kirkland, WA 98034   Ms Judy Reams

Cabrillo Doberman Pinscher Club	Nancy Heitzman	408 659-4202
Doberman Pinscher Club of No Cal	Cobbey Sova	415 595-1010
Doberman Pinscher Club of Sacramento	Adriane Woodroock	916 451-7698
Redwood Empire Doberman Pinscher Club	JoAnn Oerline	415 820-3852
San Joaquin Delta Doberman Pinscher Club	Eileen Petros	209 522-4182
Michelle Santana		415 341-5374
Sharon Asbell	Sharwill	415 457-6063
Judy Beaton		415 883-5816
Bill Goff & Don Moss	Loki	415 897-9253
Alan Or Debbe Katz	Ala-Deb	510 685-9550
Donna Irvine		
Pat Neller	Von Lieb	510 825-3215
Eve & Roger Auch	Irongate	510 932-2362
Sylvia Hammarstrom	Skansen	707 795-7070
Delores King	Lu Del	707 829-9789
Gerrie Hart	Shal-Mar	916 387-0934
Jack Or Ruth Edwards	Morgansonne	408 649-4280
Jan Todd	JT	916 342-1355

Appendix A: Local Breeders and Breed Club Directory

Dogo Argentino
Dogo Argentino Club of America, Inc
4575 Lebanon Rd Danville KY 40422   606 236-3702
Argentine Dogo Club of America
2014 Albany St Lafayette, IN 47904 ($5)
Karolyn Harris   Thunder Mt   916 991-5955

Dogue de Bordeaux
Giordano   916 421-8760

English Cocker Spaniel
English Cocker Spaniel Club of America, Inc
PO Box 252 Hales Corners, WI 53130 Mrs Kate Romanski, Sec
English Cocker Spaniel Club of Nor Cal   Richard Vanier   510 828-4576
Jeannie Bobbitt   415 386-2611
Lynne Matuk   510 228-7776
Joan Nygaard   Glenwood   510 758-5960
Richard & Karen Vanier   510 828-4576

English Setter
English Setter Assoc of America, Inc
114 S Burlington Oval Dr. Chardon OH 44024Dawn Ronyak   216 285-4531
Golden Gate English Setter Club   Linda Epperson   415 248-5808
Monterey Bay English Setter Club   MA Samuelson   408 997-2605
Gold Country English Settle Fanciers   Joyce Weichsi   916 966-6596
Jim & Sharon Dok   Castlehill   408 847-1360
Joyce Weichsl   916 966-6596

English Springer Spaniels
English Springer Spaniel Field Trial Assoc, Inc
29512 47th Ave S Auburn, WA 98001 Ms Marie Andersen, Sec
Golden Gate English Springer Spaniel   Genevieve Gallien
Santa Clara Valley Eng Springer Spaniel   Harry Carpenter   408 225-8436
Sacramento English Springer Spaniel Club   Liz Kiener   916 791-3271
English Springer Spaniel Field Trials   Ms. Marie Andersen
Margaret Mayes   707 545-8569
Ben Or Dorothy Roach   Tuckahoo   707 838-2968
Cliff Or Marge Brown   916 243-0775

English Toy Spaniel
English Toy Spaniel Club of America
18451 Sheffield Lane Bristol, IN 46507 Ms Susan Jackson, Sec
David Peters & Bj Miller   Hillcroft   510 947-2622

Entlebucher Sennenhund
Kathern Stalley   415 461-2040
Jay Delepine   510 676-8843

Field Spaniel
Field Spaniel Society of America
11197 Keystone Lowell, MI 49331 Mrs Sally Herweyer, Sec
CC Blatter   909 792-4184
Bob & Patricia Ramsey   Bel Canto   714 761-7144

Fila Brasileiro
Fila Brasileiro Club of America
244 Flat Rock Church Rd Zebulon GA 30295   706 567-8085
Sue Armstrong   Fazenda Do Indomito   916 448-5277

Finnish Spitz
Finnish Spitz Club of America
110 Knots Landing Macon, GA 31210 Mr Richard Yates, Sec
Lee Or Kathryn Bray   916 222-5719
Michele Sevryn   916 549-3303

Flat-Coated Retriever
Flat-Coated Retriever Society of America, Inc
6608 Lynwood Blvd Richfield, MN 55423 Ann Mortenson, Sec

Debbie & Gerald Field	Goodtime	209 297-0434
William Young	Springold	510 676-2009
Leslie Puppo		707 446-8581
Brenda Radcliff		916 988-2164

Fox Terrier
American Fox Terrier Club
PO Box 604 South Plainfield, NJ 07080 Mr Martin Goldstein, Sec

Fox Terrier Club of Northern Cal	Ehren Webster	415 329-1719
Donald Dresser (Wires)		209 255-2304
Thomas Keller (Smooth)		209 826-3170
Jack Or Ruth Edwards (Smooth)	Morgansome	408 649-4280
Helen Sayer Sayer (Toy)		415 388-3720
Doris Or Lawrence Weems (Toy)	Sweetwater	707 579-1435
Ruth Edwards (Smooth)		408 649-4280
Wolf (Wires)		408 438-1159
Monteyne (Wires)		415 283-5306
Ehren Webster (Wires)		415 329-1719
Rosemary Schmele (Wires)		415 493-0967
Judy Winkler (Wires)	Cullina	415 697-1921
Paul & Cynthia Pruitt (Wires)		415 726-8618
Jean Heath (Wires)		415 846-1326
Clarence Scheid (Wires)		707 448-6717
Adey May Dunnell (Smooth)		707 425-3766
Eddie Boyer (Wire)		916 272-4940
Ann Mckee (Wires)		916 448-7470
Richard Vida (Wires)		916 488-3036
Carl & Rita Burson (Smooth)		916 791-7042

Foxhound, American
America Foxhound Club
1221 Oakwood Ave. Dayton Oh 45419   Mrs. Jack Heck

Appendix A: Local Breeders and Breed Club Directory

French Bulldog
French Bulldog Club of America

1141 Constantinople New Orleans LA 70015 David Kruger		504 895-4739
Lou Carbona	Jaguar	209 291-0175
George Niles	Club Contact	209 299-3693
Joanne Williams	Gelwil	707 778-1828

German Pinscher
German Pinscher Club of America

531 Huntington Tpke Bridgeport, CT 06610	203 371-8192

German Shepherd
German Shepherd Dog Club of America, Inc

17 W Ivy Lane Englewood NJ 07631Blanche Beisswenger		
German Shephard Dog Club of NC	Dr Gloria Rice	
Diablo Valley German Shepherd Dog Club	Janice Raeburn	510 449-5133
Golden State German Shephard Dog Club	Sue Cogliandro	
German Shephard Dog Club of Sacramento	Kelly Walton	916 391-3211
Sonomarin German Shepherd Dog Club	Susan Sizemore	707 763-7706
German Shepherd Dog Club of San Jose	Pat Larsen	408 265-5584
San Joaquin Valley German Shepherd Dog Club	Jim Stacy	209 276-1478
Elaine Hodgin		209 786-2245
Mary Scheinuck		209 823-9487
Kathy Bronzini		408 720-1009
Julia Or William Ortner		408 722-1031
Dorothy Or Kathleen	Lewenhaus	415 364-8368
Dorothy Linn	Linnloch	415 591-3461
Schokrest		415 728-3647
Barbara Or Bill Ross	Talimar	510 223-8078
Beryl Eshom	Arelee	510 443-7131
Ruby Hertz	R Beth	510 569-4682
Julia Priest		510 778-1638
Meredith & Fred Noreen	Merick	510 825-5800
Robert Or Susan Sisemore	Suboja	707 763-7706
Art Sinclair	Firethorn	707 795-2035
Cappy Pottle Or Gloria Birch	Covy Pottle	707 795-6375
Lois Gregor	Schatten	707 938-3351
Nick Or Alix Moline	Riverain	707 938-4508
Erika Buckley	Tamarin	707 996-5789
Frank & Carolyn Metello		916 637-4848
Louise Penery		916 661-7407
Sharon Albright		916 878-2826
Nadine Grady		916 944-1970

German Shorthaired Pointer
German Shorthaired Club of America

1101 W Quincy Englewood CO 80110	Geraldine Irwin	
German Shorthaired Pointer Club of Cen Cal	Mary McDole	
German Shorthaired Pointer Club of Cal	Mick Fairchild	415 757-2131
German Shorthaired Pointer Club of No Cal	Debbie Ferguson	
German Shorthaired Pointer of Santa Clara Vly	Jack Halford	408 723-9326

Dog Owners Guide

San Joaquin German Shorthaired Pointer Club	Irene Merrell	805 587-6044
Sharon Asbell	Sharwill	415 457-6063
Melvyn & Ada Fairchild	Fairchild	510 757-2131
Jay Or Kathy Bodutch		707 422-3719
Mildred Reveil	Weidenbach	707 795-4797
Silke Alberts	Cadenberg	707 644-9901
Carl & Susan Kennedy		916 424-4338
Davis & Bonnie		916 961-6924

German Wirehaired Pointers

German Wirehaired Pointers Club
3838 Davison Lake Road Ortonville MI 48462 Barbara Hein

German Wirehaired Pointer Club of No Cal	Mildred Revell	707 795-4797
Doris Erlich		510 644-8068

Golden Retriever

Golden Retriever Club of America
2005 NE 78th St Kansas City, MO 64118 Ms Catherine Bird, Sec

Northern Cal Golden Retriever Club	Nancy Hopkins	510 262-0597
Charles Eagan	Glen Mist	415 283-5536
Charlotte Gaynor	Trumpet	415 334-4474
Bill Young		415 676-2009
Jane Davison	Buternut	415 897-6654
William Young	Springold	510 676-2009
Gerald Roose	Chardonnay	707 252-1659
Margaret Mayes		707 545-8569
Ann Chase		707 553-9663
Jennifer Or Erik Masterson	Masters	707 762-3670
Ron Or Linda Giorgi	Foxfire	707 778-8170
Clara Brown	Windrift	707 795-5010
Ron Akers	Ronakers	707 938-1173
Patti Or John Davis	Sunsong	707 963-2933
Jim Wood		707 963-9193
Ted Or Patty Owen		916 246-8870
Robin Baker		916 392-6766
Janet & Robert Trigg		916 686-6425
Cindy Krajanowski	Wynsak	916 893-4247

Gordon Setter

Gordon Setter Club of America
632 W El Morado Ct., Ontario, CA 91762

Golden Gate Gordon Setter Club	Nancy Thompson	916 989-1633
Norman Sorby	Springset	707 763-8276
Wendy Czarnecki	Bright Star	707 763-5735

Great Dane

Great Dane Club of America,Inc
442 Country View Lane Garland TX 75043   Marie Flint

Great Dane Club of Nothern California	Connie Hunter	209 723-8075
Nick Or Patti Mattera	Mattera	707 448-0214
Beatrice Stone	Spring Lake	707 539-2412
Pat Gurtner	Coleridge Blues	707 795-6404

110

Appendix A: Local Breeders and Breed Club Directory

John Or Janis Robak (Harlequin)	Steigerhill	707 447-7460
Vincent Or Joan Mulligan	Paradise	707 762-3864
Kimberly Or Gordon Cross	Aldawn	916 865-7018

Great Pyrenees
Great Pyrenees Club of America, Inc
Rt 1 Box 119 Midland, VA 22728 Mrs Charlotte Perry, Sec

Great Pyrenees Club of California	Moya Courtenay	510 487-9689
Jonni Gonzales	Summerwind	707 448-1115
Michael & Laura Davis		707 545-1038
Christine Palmer-Persen	Euskaldun	707 838-8587
Betty Wade	Warmack	916 652-4236

Greater Swiss Mountain Dog
Greater Swiss Mt Dog Club of America

RD 8 Box 203 Sinking Spring PA 19608	H. Summons	215 678 3631
Rick Or Bertha Noll	Suncatcher	415 488-0711

Greyhound
Greyhound Club of America
227 Hattertown Rd Newton, CT 06470 Ms Patricia Clark, Sec

Greyhound Club of Northern California	Patricia Gail Burnham	916 965-1253
Sheila Grant		707 422-1247
Jane Bulman	Point Breeze	707 224-1043

Harrier
Betty Burnell	Seaview	805 642 8758
Paul Or Karen Crary	Pacific	408 629-9269

Havanese
Sue & David Nelson	Shaggyluv	714 523-1311

Ibizan Hound
Ibizan Hound Club of the US
4312 E Nisbet Rd Phoenix, AZ 85032 Lisa Puskas, Sec

Johanna Bice	Redhill	707 838-0913

Irish Setter
Irish Setter Club of America, Inc
16717 Ledge Falls San Antonio TX 78232 Marion Pahy

Irish Setter Club of The Pacific	Dennis Wilson	510 687-3644
Irish Setter Club Of Central Cal	Sharon Hall	510 797-9832
Irish Setter Club Of Sacramento		916 421-0788
Irish Setter Club of Sacramento	Judy Ayres	209 477-3926
Bob Perry		209 239-1476
Wendy Czarnecki	Bright Star	707 763-5735
Pennie Or Clyde Terry	Terra Setters	916 533-8369

Irish Terrier
Irish Terrier Club of America
RR 3, Box 449 Bloomington, IL 61704

	Mary Roberts	310 864-5080
Irish Terrier Club of Northern Cal	Diana Martin	707 938-4698
Mark Or Sally George	Aberglen	707 938-2657
Ann Kasuboska		408 248-3119

Dog Owners Guide

Ray Ruiz		408 267-4937
Peter & Marilyn Shaw		415 453-4015
Mary O'brien		415 521-3246
Diana Martin	Begorra	707 938-4698
Patricia Lowrey		916 787-3102

Irish Water Spaniel
Irish Water Spaniel Club of America
24712 SE 380 Enumclaw, WA 98022Ms Renae Peterson, Sec
Nancy Wiley   415 461-7533

Irish Wolfhound
Irish Wolfhound Club of America
8855 US Route 40 New Carlisle, OH 45344 Mrs William Pfarrer, Sec

Northern California Irish Wolfhound ClubSuzanne McCombs		916 357-4185
Irish Wolfhound Assoc Of The West CoastLois Thomasson		408 484-1668
Maria Theresa Grotano		209 931-1549
Susan Kinloch		415 841-6401
Janet Souza		415 851-4708
Terry & Robin Burchett		510 689-9765
Robert Or Marsia Weeks	Seachtain	707 426-0753
Mike & Agnes Curtis	Tara Heights	707 823-4665
Chuck Or Arline Stockham	Knightwind	707 839-1421

Italian Greyhound
Italian Greyhound Club of America, Inc
35648 Menifee Rd Murrieta, CA 92563 Lillian Barber, Sec

Camille Bakker		408 866-2482
Carol Curry	Locar	510 686-2089
Jan Carson	Krystal	916 361-9405
Jani Johnson		916 371-2720
Nona Molaison	Jo-Na-Da	916 534-7769

Jack Russell Terrier
The Jack Russell Terrier Club of America
PO Box 23, Winchester Center, CT 06094 Holly Lestinsky   203 379-3282
Jack Russell Terrier Club of America
PO Box 365 Far Hills NJ 07931   908 234-1860
Jack Russell Terrier United World Federation

2644 Beckleysville Rd., Millers, MD 21107	Jack Batzer	410 343-1568
Liz Jenner		209 334-5971
Doris Sneider	Impressive	707 795-4900
Jean Coltrin	Porter Creek	707 942-6884

Japanese Chin
Japanese Chin Club of America
2113 Tract Rd Fairfield, PA 17320   Ms Faith Milton, Sec

Norma Thomas		415 453-8458
Robert Or Janet Jacobsen		707 525-1801
Dixie Mcculloch	Chisai	707 762-6362

112

Appendix A: Local Breeders and Breed Club Directory

Keeshond
Keeshond Club of America, Inc
8535 N 10th Ave Phoenix, AZ 85021Ms Shannon Kelly, Sec

Keeshund Club OF Northern Cal	Jane Norton	916 753-3244
Ada Wirth		916 362-1748
Vivian Toepfer	Kavalier	209 467-8014
Suzanne Orozco	Windriff	209 524-2323
Joanne Byars	Rich Bob	406 259-2001
Jimmy Kranz	Star-Kees	408 842-0451
Robin Stark	Star-Kees	408 842-0451
Gloria Marie Marcelli	Magic Myst	408 997-6104
David & Joanne Brown	Vintage	415 262-4522
Dolores Sapiro	Skannex	415 681-1712
William & Anne Bradshaw	Clayton	415 689-5948
Steven Streich	Jovan	415 897-7482
Fred & Lucy Silvey	Rebo	415 934-7589
Lewis Or Nancy Cuccia		510 233-4500
Jack & Arlene Grimes		510 372-6366
Linda & Greg Ball	Keefolk	510 455-0661
Joanne Reed	Windrift	707 538-7648
Mike & Marty Carr	Carr-Kees	707 642-2491
S Kelly	Shamrock	707 996-9472
Martha & Russell Huck	Nightwatch	916 624-8866
Joanne Reed	Windrift	916 689-1661
Jane & Donald Norton	Kee-Xote	916 753-3244
Donna Lundeen		916 885-0812
Jerry & Penny Manser		916 933-4660

Kerry Blue Terrier
United States Kerry Blue Terrier Club
2458 Eastridge Dr Hamilton, OH 45011 Ms Barbara Beuter, Sec

Kerry Blue Terrrier Club of Nor Cal	Ginny Bryant	510 455-5125
Eilen Andrade		510 232-1839
Florence Galeu	Walnut Lane	415 325-1469

Kyi-Leo

Harriet Linn	Lin-Kai	510 685-4019

Komondor
Komondor Club of America, Inc
W358 S10708 Nature Rd Eagle, WI 53119 Ms Sandra Hanson

Arthur Or Diane	Erdosi	408 867-5830

Kuvasz
Kuvasz Club of America
RR1 Box 121, Hannibal, NY 13074Ms Nancy Schefcick, Sec

Furgeson	Santa's Forest	206 793-0098
Michele Or Dan Valesano	Konocto	707 994-4746
Kyi-Leos Harriett Linn	Lin Kai	510 685-4019

Labrador Retriever

Labrador Retriever Club, Inc
9690 Wilson Mills Rd Chardon, OH 44024 Mr Chris Wincek, Sec

Golden Gate Labrador Retriever Club	Vicki Blodgett	408 429-0159
San Joaquin Valley Labrador Retriever Club	Laura Fletcher	209 523-8126
Vonnie Russell Or Lisa Daross	Hygate	209 667-1808
George Or Kathy Wussow	Bay Vue	408 286-7153
Vicki Blodgett	Delby	408 429-0159
Don & Virginia Campbell	Campbellcroftt	408 476-0759
Jan Grannemann	Janrod	408 663-6266
Ann & Paul Gamlin		415 592-8394
Steve Bectel	De Las Uvas	415 768-7600
Elaine Dal	Bon	415 892-5469
Janet Peters	Caerlon	415 897-3981
Marianne Foote	Winroc	510 447-8513
Terri Herigstad	Marstad	510 449-1584
Lou Or Pat Dutra	Briarcreek	510 676-4482
Kevin Henry	Vision	510 933-4826
Malinda Grosch	Waterproof	707 523-4582
Randi Quinn	Sundancer	707 526-9904
Jane Borders	Braemer	707 584-0154
Debbie Ziegler	Bayside	707 584-8196
Rik Or Kathleen	Rummell	916 241-7383
Kurt Or Carol Albrecht	Coalcyn	916 342-3313
B Hollandsworth	Sweethome	916 343-4209
Mary Lovell		916 421-0785
Dan Or Celia Cuellar		916 549-4623
Mary Williams		916 662-1264
Cindy Braley	Cinderhill	916 676-8908
Trudy Rose	Talimar	916 689-2549
Autumn Davidson Dvm	Clarion	916 758-9960
Esther Abshier	Two Step	916 895-0321
Anthony Peruzzi		916 938-4062

Lakeland Terrier

United States Lakeland Terrier Club
PO Box 214 Bayport, NY 11705   Ms Carol Griffin, Sec

Jean Heath	Black Witch	510 846-1326
Bernice Kossow		916 846-5304

Leonberger

Leonberger Club of America
PO Box 97 Georgetown, CT 06829

Lhasa Apsos

American Lhasa Apsos Club, Inc
18105 Kirkshire Birmingham, MI 48025 Ms Amy Andrews, Sec

Lhasa Apso Club of Northern California	Pat Keen	209 369-4388
Midge Hylton & Pat Keen	Hylan	209 369-4388
Sherry Swanson	Shojin	510 833-9251
Katherine Stone La Rue	Stonelea	707 463-1248

114

Appendix A: Local Breeders and Breed Club Directory

Maltese
American Maltese Assoc
6145 Coley Ave Las Vegas, NV 89102 Ms Pamela Rightmyer, Sec

Pauline Vieira	Chapau	209 334-1616
Len Reppond		510 562-2561
David Or Bonnie Sheals	Westwinds	707 778-1406
Carole Baldwin	Fantasyland	707 795-5151
Louise Bialek	Dunars	916 395-6449

Manchester Terrier (Toy)
American Manchester Terrier Club
52 Hampton Rd Pitttown, NJ 08867   Diane Haywood, Sec

Gerrie Hart	Shal-Mar	916 387-0934
Fred & Shirley Carnett		916 622-4149
Fred Or Myrtle Klensch	Pacificia	916 652-6998

Mastiff
Mastiff Club of America, Inc
45935 Via Esparanza Temecula, CA 92590   Carla Sanchez   714 676-1161

Cynthia & Norm Everard	Tavistock	209 338-2249
Marilyn Mcdonald		209 931-5018
Nancy Or Jerry Harvey	Middle Earth	408 663-4139
Robert Goldblatt	Goldleaf	408 763-1138
Joe Chanbant	Arbian	415 457-1861
Diane Collins	Blackpoint	415 897-3905
Margo Lauritsen		510 426-2430
Charlotte Strong	Windsor	707 433-3728
Mike & Dee Gensburger	Gulph Mills	707 763-8443
Joanne Williams	Gelwil	707 778-1828
Lynda Piercy	Wannabe Run	916 343-5171
Lance & Barbara House	Brite Star	916 477-1022
Fred & Shirley Carnett		916 622-4149
Paula Duncan		916 672-0326
Omar Herman	Tehama	916 824-4766

Mastiff, Neopolitan
United States Neapolitan Mastiff Association
920 Bonnie Lane Auburn, CA 91343

		818 892-4944
		or 609 728-8937
	Dog Star	818 767-8442
Lou Carbona	Jaguar	209 291-0175

Mastiff, Tibetan
American Tibetan Mastiff Association
920 Bonnie Lane Auburn, CA 95603

		916 888-6888
Betty Bowling		707 374-2386
Kristina Sherling	Sierra	707 744-1858

Miniature Bull Terrier
Miniature Bull Terrier Club of America
17 Fremont Rd Sandown, NH 03873   Marilyn Drewes, Sec

Sharon Duvall		916 674-9447

Miniature Pinscher

Miniature Pinscher Club of America
Rt 1 Box 173 Temple, TX 76501   Ms Kay Phillips, Sec

Patty Bartley		209 536-1512
Tony & Alice Parlangeli	Alanco	510 278-5924
Dee Chambers		510 687-2888
Cathy Hopson	Merryheart	707 963-4246
Gerrie Hart	Shal-Mar	916 387-0934
Shawn Brown	Von Hatten	916 878-0269

Newfoundland

Newfoundland Club of America
RR3 Box 155 Carlinville, IL 62626   Clyde Dunphy, Sec

DC & Georgia Basolo	Hard Tack	209 835-3259
Kendall & Diane Price		408 353-3447
Lucille & Michael Lomax	Tabu	408 484-9500
Richard & Donna Humphreys		510 757-6236
Paul Or Carol Livrament	Bonnie Bear	707 823-5677
Dale & Edie Koster	Royal Flush	916 265-6508
Julie Kelley	Lakota	916 547-4710

Norfolk Terrier

Norfolk & Norwich Terrier Club
12 W Southhampton Philadelphia PA 15317 Edward Resovsky 412 745 7070

Neil Hamilton		408 225-8397
Robin Ormiston	Kasimira	707 446-1722
Sharon Curry	Shonleh	707 823-2342
Roger & Geri Cutler		916 791-1447

Norwegian Elkhound

Norwegian Elkhound Association of America
4772 Mentzer Church Rd Convoy, OH 45832 Mrs Diane Coleman, Sec

Norwegian Elkhound Assoc of Nor Cal	Dee Queen	408 926-3123
Sacramento-Sierra Norwegian Elkhound Club		916 331-8110
David Or Bev Brown	Tyken	408 262-7368
Dee Queen	Vindarne	408 926-3123
Ed Allen	Dragon End	415 591-8056
Kathy Paquito	Norwood	510 234-1092
Mike Or Kathi Boyd	Rendition	510 625-0864
Joan Or Terri Brennan	Tiro	510 625-4123
Sandi Or Dave Smith	Telggren	707 964-1035
Sharon Graves	Bristlecone	916 268-9664
Carl Or Rita Burson	Bristlecone	916 791-7042
Ken Or Judy Strakbein	Linvicta	916 967-3237

Norwegian Lunderhund

Norwegian Lunderhund Club of America
33 Amsterdam Rd., Milford, NJ 08848 Harvey Sanderson

		908 995-7422
		or 619 246-8856
Jo Ellen Schmudlack	Nereng	818 951-2083

Appendix A: Local Breeders and Breed Club Directory

Norwich Terrier
Norwich & Norfolk Terrier Club
407 Grenoble Dr Sellersville, PA 18960 Mrs Maurice Matteson, Sec

Neil Hamilton		408 225-8397
Ed & Ann Dum	Arroyo	510 462-7776
Sharon Curry	Shonleh	707 823-2342
Ann Or Buff Buffington	Doggywood	707 994-5241
Judy Davis		916 671-2682
Earl Or Judy May		916 742-8506
Frank Burke		916 755-0241

Nova Scotia Duck Tolling Retriever

Diana Humanik	Nat Club	402 493-4411
Jacki Ledau		209 333-0829

Old English Sheepdog
Old English Sheepdog Club of America
14219 E 79th St South Derby, KS 67037 Ms Kathryn Bunnell, Sec

Old English Sheepdog League Of NoCal	Pam Henry	707 579-1848
Old English Sheepdog Club Of Sacramento	Karen Stetler	916 695-3500
Bob & Renee Crabtree	Windswept	510 793-6143
Florence Or Lowell Narron	Wiggleworth	510 846-0401
Pam Henry	Blu Mountain	707 579-1848
Famous Or Margie Holt	Dreamweaver	707 792-2395
Jan Or Holly Mcintire	Tales End	916 331-4840
Margaret Welty	Bearlight	916 677-8040
Debbie Lehr	Lazy L	916 687-7131
Karen Or Fred Stetler	Londonaire	916 695-3500
Patrick & Janet Butler	Tales End	916 969-4366
Joyce Keefer	Grey Shadow	916 985-2195

Otter Hound
Otter Hound Club of America
Rt1 Box 247 Palmyra, NE 68418 Dian Quist-Sulek, Sec

Papillon
Papillon Club of America
551 Birch Hill Rd Shoemakersville, PA 19555 Mrs Janice Dougherty, Sec

Dorothy Hageman	Wildways	707 224-1773
Mortishia Fairchild	Jem	707 552-3825
Annabelle Hofmann		805 964-2446
Dottie Boyza		916 223-5463

Pekingese
Pekingese Club of America
Rt 1 Box 321 Bergton, VA 22811 Mrs Leonie Marie Schultz, Sec

Pekingese Club of Central California	Victoria Powell	916 877-8912
Pacific Coast Pekingese Club	Carolyn Simpson	805 944-0915
Kim Langley		209 748-5589
Patty & Don Hempel		408 377-7718
Norma Thomas		415 453-8458
Lorraine Morton	Sum Fun	510 223-0633
Tuula Damon	Finnfair	707 795-3038
Lois Thomas	Ai-Kou	916 687-7249

Dog Owners Guide

Petit Basset Griffon Vendeen
Petit Basset Griffon Vendeen Club of America
426 Laguna Way Simi Valley, CA 93065 Ms Shirley Knipe, Sec
Marianne Paulsson or Ruth Balladone   Balmar   707 823-4543

Pharoah Hound
Pharoah Hound Club of America
Rt 209 Box 285 Stone Ridge NY 12484 Rita Sacks 914 687 9200
Libby Leone   Lileo   408 663-2550
Don Delmore   510 865-9418

Pointer, American
American American Pointer Club
Rt 1 Box 10 Branch, LA 70516   Ms Lee Ann Stagg, Sec
Cindy Krajanowski   Kynsak   916 893-4247

Pomeranian
American Pomeranian Club
2514 Custer Pky Richardson, TX 75080 Mrs Harold Kinne, Sec
Northern California Pomerian Club   Rachael Capps   209 233-7818
Dolly Trauner   Phyner   415 346-5314
Marge Kranzfelder   Forever Yours   415 572-0149
Kutilek   415 872-1795
Jeff Greer   Fiddler Green   415 892-9632

Poodle
Poodle Club of America
S. New Boston Rd. Box 211 Francestown NH 03043 Mrs. Richard Kiczek
Poodle Club of Central California   Janet Collins   707 867-3607
Poodle Mission Trails Poodle Club   Rita Perko   415 858-1111
Ann Or Katherine Kennedy (Toy)   Clarion   209 368-9069
Roberta Stone (Min)   Stonewood   415 892-3191
Florence Graham (Std)   Graphic   415 479-4229
Roberta Stone (Toy)   Stonewood   415 892-3191
Gloria Mackay & K Wintroath   Glory   510 778-1239
Ingeborg Sesenschin (Min)   Midnight Miniatures   707 425-5005
Robin Miler (Min, Toy)   Cantata   707 664-8624
Irene Guerds (Toy)   Cherwilene   707 795-1002
Gail Zamora (Toy)   Zamora   916 268-3201
Joan Smith   916 624-4156

Portuguese Water Dog
Portuguese Water Dog Club of America
176 Beech St Islip, NY 11751   Ms Virginia Santoli, Sec
David Or Cheryl Smith   Dacher   408 358-2136
Lorraine Carver   Sete Mares   707 763-3477
Lisa Hubbart   Alto Mare   707 778-3430
Rebecca Morin   916 987-0537

Appendix A: Local Breeders and Breed Club Directory

Pug
Pug Dog Club of America

1820 Shadowlawn St Jacksonville, Fl 32205Blanche Roberts		818 703-5026
Northern California Pug Club	Donelle Richards	408 726-1543
Jerry & Mary Ortel		209 836-5138
George Or Kathy Wussow	Bay Vue	408 286-7153

Puli (Hungarian)
Puli Club of America

5109 Kathy Way Livermore, CA 94550 Ms Barbara Stelz, Sec		510 449-4190
Puli Club of Northern California	Carson Haines	
Barbara Or Nancy Prydain		408 354-0726
Arthur Or Diane Erdosi		408 867-5830
Barbara Stelz	Tordor	707 778-8126

Rat Terrier
Rat Terrier Club of Southern California

Loyal Penicks	714 737-6446

Rhodesian Ridgeback
Rhodesian Ridgeback Club of the United States

PO Box 121817 Ft Worth, TX 76121 Ms Betty Epperson, Sec

Linda Batson	Deer Ridge	408 688-2242
Gerlinde Pruyn		415 634-7921
Gerlinde Staub	Hundelridge	510 526-7092
Clayton Or Cheri	Camelot	510 526-9424
Theresa Bowermaster	Sierra Ridge	510 634-2290
Lisa Sullivan	Miramar	510 803-9621
David Bueno & Gregory Castillo		510 935-4758
Marge Nobles	Vine Ridge	707 578-0999
Diane Jacobsen	Calico Ridge	707 829-0768
Chuck & Mary Bononi	Copper Ridge	916 365-0872

Rottweiler
American Rottweiler Club

PO Box 992053, Redding, CA 96099	Denise Sisneroz	916 241-7388
Associated Rottweiler Fanciers of NC	Robert & Pat Baston	510 569-2252
Western Rottweiler Owners	Karen Aguayo	510 373-6877
Jerry Or Deanna Warkentin	Obstgarden	209 591-5828
James Turner Jr	Kalimba	209 661-8290
Bruce Or Mary Mishler	Bramis	209 833-9002
Adrian Or Charles Pareles	Pretorian	209 875-0605
Joy Hess		209 962-4455
Bruce Or Mary Beth Femmel	Crosswinds	408 749-0125
Dee Hernandez		408 848-2101
Janet Or Nelson Davis	Ja-Nel	408 997-5433
Pene Johnson		415 229-0684
Hildegard / Franz Mikoleit	Vom Sonnenhaus	415 347-5121
Laurie Schwemberger	Von Scwartzwald	415 359-6810
Ken Or Hildegard Griffin		415 897-3888
Linda Lopez	Von Schonheit	510 235-9553
Danielle Green	Granhaus	510 254-2074

Victoria Cochran	Imaygo	510 284-1882
Keith Or Charlotte Twinehan	Medeahs	510 471-4049
Kristy Peixoto		510 537-9193
Kim Waite		510 625-1360
Peter Or Diane Meier	Shadow Dance	510 846-4309
Carol Beasky	Ikon	510 930-8445
Ren Neville		707 275-0433
Wes Or Linda Cassidy	Weslin	707 528-1241
Susan Guaragua		707 570-2281
Jc Cardillo-Lee		707 778-7575
Brian & Patricia Ciocci		707 778-8739
Ann & George Goring	Von Stalker	707 795-6766
Pam Porterfield		707 829-2456
Bryan Or Loralei Dewe	Dewe	707 829-7688
Gigi Couch		707 839-4253
Denise Sisnerez	Gipfel	916 241-7388
Colleen Feaster		916 334-1321
Frestani		916 342-6216
Cheryl Britton	River Rutt	916 458-8953
Harry Or Gloria Bishop	Von Eppo	916 474-1808
Gavin Slabbert	Ebony Ranch	916 652-7687
Janice Stannard	JW Ka-Har	916 652-9112
Brent Wolfe		916 678-5651
Marlene Lorie	Marlo	916 791-2440
Lois Montgomery	Hi Hills	916 823-0212
Gary Or Roberta Martin	Roma	916 891-5639

Saluki

Saluki Club of America
Po Box 753 Mercer Island, WA 98040 Marilyn LaBrache Brown, Sec

Saluki Club of Greater San Francisco	Nancy Olson-Close	209 463-1965
Vicki Or Warren		408 688-7508
Lesley Brabyn	Timaru	415 381-2534
Sandra Wornum		415 924-7020
Sam Or Margaret Smith		916 246-7341
Mary Ellen Gorske		916 343-2414

Samoyed

Samoyed Club of America
W6434 Francis Rd Cascade, WI 53011 Kathie Lensen, Sec

Northern California Samoyed Fanciers	Luvera Morgan	510 223-9150
John & Evelyn Coloma	Mauna-Kea	408 842-3329
Gail S Spieker	Rossia	415 325-8115
Bonnie Giffin	Bykhal	415 349-1367
Terry & Gail Campbell	Tega	510 278-2275
Ralph & Robin Gowen	Orion	510 672-9223
Marilyn & Derek Gitelson	Sansaska	510 676-2268
Tammy & Jim Lynch	Firecloud	707 422-1901
Homer & Jeanne Zwuer	Snowcastle	707 464-1337
Donna Tappan	Golden Light	707 579-0131
Gerald & Nancy Sevigny		916 971-2244

Appendix A: Local Breeders and Breed Club Directory

Schipperke

Schipperke Club of America
5205 Chaparral Laramie, WY 82070   Ms Diana Dick, Sec

Lori Mcculland		702 673-4040
Shirley Emmons	Dee Po	707 224-4192
Nancy Taylor	Seaworthy	916 446-9275
Genia Boshion		916 474-3683
Esther Abshier	Two Step	916 895-0321

Schnauzer, Miniature

American Miniature Schnauzer Club
RR2 Box 3570 Bartlesville, OK 74003 Mrs Susan Atherton, Sec

Min Schnauzer Club of Northern Cal	Milly Robertson	415 591-9918
Min Schnauzer Club of Northern Cal	Larry & Georgia Drivon	209 931-5671
Min Schnauzer Club of Northern Cal	Margaret Doty	408 736-1293
Min Schnauzer Club of Northern Cal	Joan Wieder	415 924-9787
Min Schnauzer Club of Northern Cal	Glendora Norwood	707 762-5898
Min Schnauzer Club of Northern Cal	Beverly Pfaff	707 864-0606
Min Schnauzer Club of Northern Cal	Cheryl Mazzoncini	916 724-3218
Gerald Mcintosh		209 266-5330
Nadine Wright		209 462-5953
Russel Weaver Or David Wotham	Ardee	209 462-7333
Mary Alford		209 532-8788
Don Scott		209 545-3977
Barbara Strand		209 667-4477
Maxine Roster		209 736-4942
Pat Gerling		209 823-0927
Larry Or Georgia Drivon		209 931-5671
Lu Vidak		408 724-6657
Margaret Doty	Camelot	408 736-1293
Judy Sousa		408 867-4279
Linda Watkins		415 591-9317
Milly Robertson		415 591-9918
Joan Wieder		415 924-9787
Jan Heffron		707 545-2610
Bob Or Dolores Featherer		707 745-0190
Glendora Norwood	Glendora	707 762-5898
Sylvia Hammarstrom	Skansen	707 795-7070
Joni Cookston	Enjoy Ebony Acre	707 823-0300
Beverly Pfaff	Jebema	707 864-0606
Dan Durigan	Fairwind	707 864-2042
Brenda Couey	Carlena	707 928-4350
Marilyn Nichols		916 332-1178
Chris Mays		916 622-9443
Bill Or Amelia Baltrausaitis		916 633-4362
Cheryl Mazzoncini	Dunnigan	916 724-3218
Minnie Kelly		916 771-0592
Patricia Or Sarah O'brien	Emerald Isle	916 782-1418

Dog Owners Guide

Schnauzer, Standard
Standard Schnauzer Club of America
4 Deerfield, CT 06804   Ms Kathy Donovan, Sec
Standard Schnauzer Club of Nor Cal   Mary Lou Just   209 982-1920
Joan Sitton   Highlands   408 625-3061
Sylvia Hammerstrom   707 795-7070

Schnauzer, Giant
Giant Schnauzer Club of America
4220 S Wallace Chicago, IL 60609 Ms Dorothy Wright, Sec
Sacramento Valley Giant Schnauzer Club   916 967-4522
Glendora Norwood   Glendora   707 762-5898
Marilyn Casstevens   Springstaff   707 792-1797

Scottish Deerhounds
Scottish Deerhound Club of America
545 Cummings Lane Cottontown, TN 37048 Mrs Joan Shagan, Sec
Judd Case & A Babitch   Sindar   510 676-5054

Scottish Terrier
Scottish Terrier Club of America
PO Box 1893 Woodinville, WA 98072 Ms Diane Zollinger, Sec
San Francisco Bay Scottish Terrier Club   Dan Graves   408 453-6483
Fredcoch   408 226-0511
Peggy & Jerry Burge   408 238-2327
Lynn Huffaker   Kellscot   415 892-9501
Joseph Penden   Jospen   707 778-9229
Phyllis Dabbs   Stoncroft   805 871-2736

Sealyham Terrier
American Sealyham Terrier Club
Box 76 Sharon Center, OH 44274 Mrs Barbara Carmany, Sec

Shar-Pei
Chinese Shar-Pei Club of America
PO Box 113809 Anchorage, AK 99511 Ms Jocelyn Barker, Sec
Shar-Pei Club of Sacramento   916 454-0278
Carol Cretser   Shaanxi   209 575-1717
Scott Or Sue Ohara   Ohara's   408 224-4185
JJ Sterling   Sterling   415 566-5654
Bertha Martin   Tai Seng   510 634-3144
Dan Or Marie Balsey   Kan Tung   510 828-6237
Bob Or Betty Barr   Barr Ridge   916 347-0209
James & Karen Hurvey   916 451-5078
Jerry Or Maureen Henderson   Como-J   916 529-2975
Mary Deitz   House Of Sam   916 925-7355
Betty Seamans   Bj's Cottage   916 991-0223

Shetland Sheepdog
American Shetland Sheepdog Association
2125 E 16th Ave Post Falls, ID 83854 Ms Susan Beacham, Sec
Sacramento Shetland Sheepdog Club   Tamra Collier   916 363-6646
Central California Shetland Sheepdog Club   Sue Lewelling   209 292-5604

122

Appendix A: Local Breeders and Breed Club Directory

Shetland Sheepdog Club of Northern Cal	Mark Hersman	209 239-5321
Mark Or Angela Hersman		209 239-5321
Corky Mariani		209 941-8026
Kathy Trevino		209 982-5413
Johanna Primeaux		408 353-3534
Kathryn & Donald Coon	Caitlin	408 723-1982
Peggie Or Ronnie Phelps		415 682-5597
Jane Bulman	Kiawa	707 224-1043
Sheryl Yu	Fairwyn	707 429-0991
Charles Or Jan Warziniack	Hiho	707 527-8115
Sharron Johnstone		707 745-2634
Chris Meneley	Westwind	707 795-1948
Louise Siri	Mystic Isle	707 795-3163
Pam Baxter		707 795-3336
Dr Stanley Levine	Sunndell	707 939-0336
Mike Or Cindy Belmont		916 275-4423
Valerie Daniels		916 626-3895
Carl & Patty Stinner		916 626-6160
Dianna Cummings	E'dees	916 644-5654
Susan Bentley		916 795-2480
Jacki Scarborough		916 961-9276
Tamie Gabrielson		916 991-7701

Shiba-Inu

National Shiba Club of America
101 Peaceful Dr Converse, TX 78109 Frances Thorton, Sec

Christopher Ross	Mokelumne	209 369-3473
Dorothy Warren	Ranch Lake	408 867-2467
Bill Goff & Don Moss	Loki	415 897-9253
Lee Or Kathryn Bray		916 222-5719

Shih Tzu

American Shih Tzu Club
837 Auburn Ave Ridgewood, NJ 07450JoAnn Regelman, Sec

Golden Gate Shih Tzu Fanciers	Sally Vilas	510 276-5521
Margaret & Frank Rukavina		209 727-5767
Katherine Stone La Rue	Stonelea	707 463-1248

Shiloh Shepherd

Russ & Judy McElroy	McElroy	909 272-9850
Gwyn Poor	Lla-Ess's	818 352-3078

Siberian Husky

Siberian Husky Club of America
18 Greenwood St Elkton, MD 21921 Ms Barbara Palmer, Sec

Northern California Siberian Husky Club	Cheri Borromeo	415 388-0329
Bay Area Siberian Husky Club		
Sheila Kuesthardt	Wodka	209 524-7631
Sherry Galka	Kolyma	209 838-8655
Jo Or Karl Geletich		209 838-3463
Mike & Jean Levine	Krista	209 838-8655
Linda Mullen	Tahluu	408 426-2151

123

Dog Owners Guide

B Sue Adams	Asanlar	408 688-6867
Raymond & Catherine Reck	Siber Kahn	408 733-7919
Sharon Osharow		415 355-1858
Cheri Borromeo	Tamasea	415 388-0329
Kevin Wright	Shunka	415 388-4365
Amara Mccarthy	Suunar	415 868-9238
Donna Beckman	Mistral	510 524-9950
Arthur & Marilyn Lassagne	Lassky	510 820-1162
Barbara Schaefer		510 947-5704
Lynne Dagan	Seeonee	707 252-6357
Pam Meek	Sakima	707 526-3233
Daniel Or Seanapowell		916 244-7235
Gene & Karen Stinson	Selestia	916 823-7546
Michele Sevryn		916 549-3303
Greg & Terry Lichtenberger	Shaddai	916 626-9699
Sam & Michelle Terry	Sangilak	916 684-7161
Ken & Robin Koop	Timberline	916 991-0542

Silky Terrier
Silky Terrier Club of America
2783 S Saulsbury St Denver, CO 80227 Ms Louise Rosewell, Sec

Silky Terrier Club of Northern California	Ivy Rogers	510 222-8240
Gd Wojtek	Elfinsilk	408 225-6247
Ivy Rogers	Jenini	510 222-8240
JJ Hicks	Houzabout	510 537-2359
Elinor Francesechi	Wexford	707 938-3792
Rl Little		916 272-6521
Hj Bialek	Dunar	916 395-6449

Skye Terriers
Skye Terrier Club of America
11567 Sutters Mill Circle Gold River, CA 95670 Mrs Karen Sanders, Sec

Walter & Carol Sumonds	Rover Run	415 897-1144
Nona Molaison	Jo-Na-Da	916 534-7769
Judy Davis	Talkan	916 674-2682

Soft Coated Wheaten Terrier
Soft Coated Wheaten Terrier Club of America
4607 Willow Lane Nazareth, PA 18064 Mrs Mary Anne Dallas, Sec

Soft-Coated Wheaten Terrier Club of NC	Jean Burke	415 941-9077
Susan Strange	Carlinayer	209 367-8861
Elaine & Bob Nerrie	Hullabaloo	415 327-4830
Brian & Mary Daily	Erindale	415 892-4992
Coralie Murry		415 924-9428
Glen & Robyn Alexander	Derryhumma	510 526-7948
Richard Or Sonya Urquhart	Marque	707 446-7494
Nancy Mcguire	Glenantrim	707 823-3667

Spinoni Italiano
Spinoni Club of America
P O Box 307 Warsaw VA 22572   Jim Channon   804 333 0309

Appendix A: Local Breeders and Breed Club Directory

St. Bernard

St Bernard Club of America
719 East Main St Belleville, IL 62220Ms Carol Wilson, Sec

St. Bernard Club of San Jose	Jan Fleener	
St. Bernard Club of Pacific Coast	Penny Mahon	707 996-4319
Sacramento Sierra St Bernard Club	Styron Pool	916 885-6304
Howard Dees		209 745-1224
Mike Or Yvonne Brophy	Mandy	707 838-9263
Penny Mahon	Belyn	707 996-4319
Skee & Shirley Tsagris	Kings Row	916 677-2369
Styron & Birthia Pool	Lucky Thirteen	916 885-6304

Staffordshire Bull Terrier

Staffordshire Bull Terrier Club
PO Box 70213 Knoxville, TN 37918 Linda Barker, Sec

Sussex Spaniel

Sussex Spaniel Club of America
908 Cowan Dr Columbia, MO 65203 Mrs Barbara Barnard, Sec

Tibetan Spaniel

Tibetan Spaniel Club of America
29W028 River Glen Rd West Chicago, IL 60185 Ms Shirley Howard, Sec

John & Angelee Fargo	Charisma's	707 795-9103
Jacki Scarborough	Sierra	916 721-3647

Tibetan Terrier

Tibetan Terrier Club of America
127 Springlea Dr Winfield, WV 25213 Ms Brenda Brown, Sec

G Scott Parsons		415 892-3418
Anne Keleman	Tisong	415 897-7431
Jeanette Or Jerry Chaix	Ragalia	707 887-7616

Tosa, Japanese

TOSA of America
9707 Noble Ave North Hills CA 91343   818 892-4944
International Tosa-Ken Association
8949 Herrick Ave, Sun Valley, CA 91352   818 768-0691

Toy Fox Terrier

Toy Fox Terrier Club of America

111 Moose Dr. Crosby TX 77532	Douglas Gordon	713 324 4269
Kay Chenoweth		415 538-8293
Olen Nichols		510 370-7748

Vizsla

Vizsla Club of America
PO Box 639 Stevensville, MO 21666 Ms Patricia Carnes, Sec

Lone Cypress Vizsla Club of Monterey	Mary Carpenter	408 624-5553
Central California Vizsla Club	Michele Coburn	805 831-5049
Vizsla Club of Northern California	Jan Simer	415 830-1361
Jenni Woodside	Matra	510 376-7865
Kirsten & Robert Schick		510 706-7012
Connie Johnson		702 323-3822
Marian Sears	Csardas	707 795-8433
Tom Ot Ginny Hanson	Szebb Vadasz	916 894-8110

Dog Owners Guide

Weimaraner
Weimaraner Club of America
PO Box 110708 Nashville TN 37222 | Dorthy Derr
Sacramento Valley Weimaraner Club | Carla Powers | 916 723-7340
Sacramento Valley Weimaraner Club | Debra Hopkins | 916 723-7340
Diane Brown | | 209 245-4296
Kathy Dunn | | 415 635-3821
Arlene Marshrey | Windwalker | 702 972-7804
Genevieve Day | | 707 838-6088
Debra Hopkins | | 916 723-7340
Vern Or Carla Powers | | 916 992-1389

Welsh Springer Spaniel
Welsh Springer Spaniel Club of America
4225 N 147th St Brookfield, WI 53005 Ms Karen Lyle, Sec
Emily Preston | | 408 683-2659
Tom & Joyce Tracy | Abbeywood | 707 546-8763

Welsh Terrier
Welsh Terrier Club of America
200 Hazelmere Dr Richmond, VA 23236 Mrs Marge McClung, Sec
Mary Smith Or Peter Kirkwood | Terwyn | 707 823-2053
Mark Or Sally George | Aberglen | 707 938-2657
Frank Burke | | 916 755-0241

West Highland White Terrier
West Highland White Terrier Club of America
33101 44th Ave NW Stanwood, WA 98292 Mrs Anne Sanders, Sec
SF Bay West Highland White Terrier Club | Marta Thompson | 209 299-2457
Harry Or Ellen Shorey | Jen-Hart | 209 224-6848
Roger & Brenda Delight | Delight's | 707 571-1877
Mark Or Sally George | Aberglen | 707 938-2657
Pat Winans | | 916 423-1302
Rita Iwamura | | 916 673-1618
Bill Or Jeanne Curtis | | 916 673-6618
Frank Burke | | 916 755-0241

Whippet
American Whippet Club
14 Oak Circle Charlottesville, VA 22901 Mrs Harriett Nash Lee, Sec
Lou Carbona | Jaguar | 209 291-0175
G Scott Parsons | | 415 892-3418
Carol Curry | Locar | 510 686-2089
Cindy Winter | | 707 485-0659
Michael Stone | | 916 742-1617

Wirehaired Pointing Griffon
Wirehaired Pointing Griffon Club
11739 SW Beaverton Hwy. 201 Beaverton OR 97005 | 503 629 5707

Appendix A: Local Breeders and Breed Club Directory

Yorkshire Terrier

Yorkshire Terrier Club of America
PO Box 100 Porter, ME 04068   Mrs Betty Dullinger, Sec

Yorkshire Terrier Club of Northern Cal	Betty Cabrera	510 846-8064
Pauline Vieira	La-Bel-Esprit	209 334-1616
Terri Or John Shumsky	Vassar Square	707 539-8024
Carole Baldwin	Fantasyland	707 795-5151
Cathy Hopson	Merryheart	707 963-4246
Dolores Kauffman		916 637-4143
Robert Webster		916 674-2239
Betty Arch	Kel-Lyn	916 776-1680

Appendix B
Rescue Contacts

A number of individual dog lovers volunteer their time to rescue purebred and mixed bred dogs from shelters and homes where owners are unable to live up to, or deal successfully with, the responsibility of dog care. Rescue individuals will make sure the dog is spayed or neutered and receives any necessary shots or medical care prior to placement. If you would like a purebred dog and would like to forego the mixed blessing of puppy raising, consider adopting a dog by calling a rescue worker.

The vast majority of rescue workers are hard working, ethical individuals who work to save dogs for little or no return financially for their efforts other than the joy of saving a life. They will charge a fee, but the fee is to recover the out-of-pocket expense associated with the rescue. A resonable fee is usually less than $100, although medical treatment sometimes raises the cost. If you are charged a large amount, ask for reciepts.

Reputable rescue individuals:

Have developed close ties with area shelters and they are contacted when a purebred dog becomes available.

Screen potential adopters for a good match between home/dog.

Keep names of qualified potential adopters on a waiting list.

Network with breed clubs and other rescuers.

Charge the new owner only the sum necessary to recapture costs and never look to profit personally from the transaction.

Never switch individuals to purebred puppies they have bred.

Foster dogs in their home while others act as a referral and directs potential adopters to a home or shelter where the dog is available.

Will not relinquish a dog that has not been spay or neutered and will not refer any potential owner to an intact male/female owner.

Owners Note: If you find yourself in a frustrating situation and you are thinking of relinquishing your dog, first seek the help of a trainer or behaviorist. Many problems can be solved by applying simple behavior modification techniques.

If anyone has a compliment or a complaint regarding a rescue individual or if you would like to join the rescue effort, please contact Nancy Lyon at the Ohlone Humane Society, PO Box 5118, Fremont, CA 94537 510 490-4587, or Canine Learning Center, PO Box 2010, Carlsbad, CA 92018

Asterisk (*) following a listing denotes rescue on behalf of breed club affiliation.

Affenpinscher
No breed rescue known. Contact local or national club

Afghan Hound
Susan Netboy		415 851-7812
Betty Leson		415 898-1502
Sandra Wornum		415 924-7020
Rose Upper		707 546-5610
Betsy Hufnagel		707 894-4007 *

Airedale Terrier
Patty Gregg		209 847-1633
Marsha Sarkisian		408 865-0779 *

Akita (Japanese)
Cindy Bualbaugh	Ref	408 262-1564
Carol Lee Ref		408 356-5905
Larry Or Robin		
La Course	Ref	408 722-3121
Carol Foti		415 488-0886
Susan Or Mark Manning		415 756-5590 *
Linda Wroth		510 223-2135
Susan Duncan	Coordinator	707 448-7643 *
Morticia Fairchild		707 552-3825
Teri Arima		916 961-8835

Alaskan Malamute
Nancy Guadagria		209 835-7445
Susie Or Al Richardson		209 835-8524
Bill & Debbie Griffith		408 365-0934
Nick Matulich		408 379-7253
Barbara Or Norm Weinstein		415 851-0648
Lani Knowlton	Ref	510 357-2487
Wendy Corr	Ref	510 538-1529

American Eskimo
No breed rescue known. Contact local or national club

American Foxhound
Paul Or Karen Crary   408 629-9269 *

American Pitbull Terrier
Ellen Prior   408 227-2273
Judy Landy   408 373-3747

American Staffordshire Terrier
Ellen Prior   408 227 2273
Judy Landy   408 373-3747

American Water Spaniel
Lorna Pumphrey   209 476-0411
Nancy Wiley   Coordinator   415 461-7533

Anatolian Shepherd
Catherine De La Cruz   707 829-1655
Janice Or James Frasche   916 488-2707

Argentine Dogo
Karolyn Harris   916 991-5955

Australian Cattle Dog
Lee Wise   209 754-4878 *
Lynda Locke   Also Acd Mix   415 573-5245
Pat Cook, Ref   510 531-8996
Marge Blankenship   707 643-6604
Liz Or Russ Evans   Ref   707 778-6689 *
Eleanor Francheschi   Ref   707 938-3792

Australian Kelpie
Connie Ruys   209 532-0209

Australian Shepherd
Laura Cox   408 262-7233
Dot Carden   510 651-0100
Ascoa   800 892-ASCA

Australian Terrier
Robbie Ryse Or Susan   415 897-5892
Sandra Lassen   Coordinator   707 876-3136
Darlene Evans   707 876-3136

Basenji
Jennifer Vargas   408 377-3477
Margaret Hof   Ref   415 453-2510 *
Kenneth & Marilyn Leighton   510 846-5300

Basset Hound
Pat Pineda   510 438-9282
Linda Moore   707 642-8690 *
Clare Hartman   916 988-6225

Dog Owners Guide

Beagle
Mary Or Trudy	408 244-1840
Paul Or Karen Crary	408 629-9269 *
Daryl Edmundson	510 935-1564 *

Bearded Collie
Ann Allen	415 381-1440
Mary Jo Kopp	415 871-7660 *

Bedlington Terrie
No breed rescue known. Contact local or national club.

Belgian Malinois
Dot Kutlin	209 368-1456
Ellen Or James Bond	408 946-2136
Margery Riddle, Ref	415 332-2838
Kris Stauffer	415 365-5613
Shelly Monson	415 648-7848
Debbi Suggs	707 629-3645
Stephanie Burns	707 996-0280
Daryle Or Cheryl Louie	916 331-4618

Belgian Sheepdog
Ann Lenardon	209 368-1456
Laura Bellows	415 381-1931
Ellen Haro	916 678-3888

Belgian Tervuren
Suzanna Brabant	415 728-7138
Sue Pokart	510 797-4347
Kyla Smay	707 527-5527
Lisa Lee, 2nd Contact	707 542-2216
Sandee Snyder	707 778-1129

Bernese Mountain Dog
Gerrel Page	415 456-3933
Ginny Gjedsted	415 469-8480
Martin Or Barbara Packard	415 941-0343
Helen Klebanoff	510 232-1617

Bichon Frise
Loree Levy	408 266-1221
Joan Cresci	510 934-0389

Black and Tan Coonhound
No breed rescue known. Contact local or national club

Bloodhound
Loree Levy	408 266-1221
Joan Cresci	510 939-9279

Border Collies
Lynda Locke	415 573-5245
Loretta Maddox, Ref	510 236-7711
Pat Cook	510 531-8996

Border Terrier
Paula Martin		510 234-2239
Cathy Kaiser		707 523-0851

Borzoi (Russian Wolfhound)
Edna Ogata		415 325-8940
Sandra Wornum		415 924-7020
Ellen Green		510 657-6135
Pat Berry		510 845-5289

Boston Terrier
Nancy Ford		408 252-0598
Loree Levy		408 266-1221
Pat Pineda		510 438-9282
Laura Hart		916 756-9232

Bouvier des Flandres
Loree Levy		408 266-1221
Laura Calhoun	2nd Contact	916 676-1538
Pam Green		916 756-2997
Susan Digiorno		916 933-0142

Boxer
Rose Fullen		209 584-6714
Andrea Jackman		408 224-4703
Carol Peck		415 355-4197
Marilyn Baum		415 383-1062
Paula Johnson		510 484-4075
Doug or Libby Campbell		510 797-6468
Wendy Morawski		707 644-7327 *

Briard
Marsha Or Dennis Gough		916 533-5079
Chuck Christianson		707 869-9090

Brittany Spaniel
Cindy Snow		408 224-0104 *
Frieda Rose	South Bay	408 942-3359
John Myers		415 493-7524
Rhonda Carlson	1st Contact	510 490-6253

Brussels Griffon
Joan Guest		415 375-8393
Olivia Litz		415 593-5592
Pat Hamann		510 234-4146

Bulldog
Linda Stonehocker		209 858-4237 *
Ellen Prior		408 227-2273
Patsy Ropp	Coordinator	408 356-0039 *
Judy Landy		408 373-3747
Mary Aiken		415 344-0273 *
Betty Hatton		415 344-0273 *
Lynda Pelovsky	1st Contact	510 483-8433 *

133

Pam Cardenas		707 429-0438 *
Patty Rungo	Sac Club	916 966-4012 *

Bullmastiff
Susan Borg		415 588-2327
Carolyn Young		916 678-2466

Bull Terrier
Troy Or Nancy Gardner	Cnt Vly	209 748-2715 *
Jayne Abelar	South Bay	408 370-3294 *
Denisa Or Alan Kajita	South Bay	408 741-0533 *
Nick Ratkovich	North Bay	415 366-1962 *
Shari Mann	SF, Coordinator	415 564-9335 *
Marguerite Neumann	North Bay	415 892-6500 *
Kevin Mcgown	East Bay	510 642-2822 *
Bill Or Cathy May	East Bay	510 676-3443 *
Bonnie Erwin	North Bay	707 823-9085 *
Don Or Karen Bates	Sacramento	916 921-1918 *
Melinda Hutchings	Sacramento	916 992-1432 *

Cairn Terrier
Dave Or Judy Meyers	Monterey	408 422-1337 *
Lynn Hicky	South Bay	408 842-7266 *
Susan Bruno	East Bay	408 842-7266 *
Bobbi Walker	Coordinator	415 388-6708 *
Nancy Bean	Sacramento	916 725-2264 *

Cavalier King Charles Spaniel
Sue Seden	South Bay	408 439-9951
Donna Kube	Monterey	408 684-0347
Bill Full	San Jose	408 984-8694 *
Dale Martin	San Francisco	415 552-0939
Dorothy Wolfe	San Mateo	415 697-3653
Ronnie Cadam	San Francisco	415 759-9813
Carol Wolf-Setka	Marin	415 883-5669
Carolyn Green	East Bay	510 376-4381
Marilyn Hill	East Bay	510 799-2682
Gayle Flander	Sacramento	916 758-2218

Chesapeake Bay Retriever
Nancy Lowenthal	Ref	415 388-2173

Chihuahua
Flo Bell	1st Contact	707 525-9575 *
Pat Porreca	Tracy/Livermore	209 836-9021 *
Sharon Hermosilo	South Bay	408 279-4444 *
Karen Abe	San Mateo/Sf	415 728-5015 *
Jill Or Bill Green	East Bay	510 827-1880 *
Shirley Emmons	North Valley	707 224-4192 *
Roberta Woodward	North Bay	707 525-9575 *
Flo Bell	1st Contact	707 525-9575 *
Rose Upper	North Bay	707 546-5610 *
Elaine Pardee	Santa Rosa	707 58-3655 *

Famous Or Margie Holt	North Bay	707 792-2395 *
Judy Padgug	Sacramento	916 992-1771 *

Chinese Crested

Alan Segal		408 663-3235
Sandra Kimmerlin-Miller	Ref	510 933-6680

Chow Chow

Ellen Prior		408 228-2273 *
Harriet Beck	Ref	415 728-9218
Prudence Baxter		707 664-9248 *

Clumber Spaniel

Janice Staples		408 265-9307
Gina Orcutt		408 776-1154
Paula Or Marla		415 589-3168 *
Flo Bell		707 525 9575

Cocker Spaniel

Ann Norton	Ref	415 873-5063*
Barbara & Joann		510 525-8533
Barbara Junior		510 528-2490

Collie

Cindy Weiner	Central Vly	209 668-2535 *
Marilyn Mothersill	S Bay Ref	408 629-2921 *
Ginny Whittman	South Bay	408 779-0670 *
Kathy Lovig	Smooths Only	510 778-7130
Jean Roberts	1st Contact	707 252-2134 *
Joanne Hawkins	North Bay	707 995-9244 *
Mike Or Becky Laspina	Sac	916 989-3885 *

Corgi, Cardigan Welsh

Debbie Oliver		408 272-2715

Corgi, Pembroke Welsh

Carol Barlick	South Bay	408 252-3259 *
Debbie Oliver	Coordinator	408 272-2715 *
Sally Howe	South Bay	408 378-7346*
Pwc Club		408 727-2715 *
Gertrude Mclaren	Peninsula	415 322-2906 *
Joan Jensen	Sf	415 474-4498 *
Marty Downing	Contra Costa	510 685-3685 *
Ilona Peckham	East Bay	510 797-1957 *
Ida Anderson	North Bay	707 224-6886 *
Joan Gibson Reid	Sacramento	916 689-1661 *
Terry Hansen	Sacramento	916 743-7753 *

Curly-Coated Retriever

Marsha Badella		510 489-9305

Dachshund

Marigene Balogh		408 253-8153
Valerie Christiansen		415 364-6288

Dog Owners Guide

Elbert Or Elizabeth Benjamin		510 223-1581 *
Debbie Darnell		510 276-6608
Flo Bell		707 525-9575
Roberta Woodward		707 525-9575
Art Grundish Or Kim Wetch		707 585-9222 *
Greta Roberts		408 247-3789 *
Sharon Or Robert Jadick		510 682-7844 *
Susan Kramer		916 726-0907 *
Darly Or Art		916 877-6010 *

Dalmatian
Lois Gregg	Central Valley	209 239-7089 *
Janina Paul	Monterey	408 847-4442 *
Club Hot Line		415 281-0542 *
Joe Cabell		415 323-6250
Linda Fish	South Bay/Sf	415 591-6202 *
Gladys Cox	East Bay	510 724-8831
Camilla Gray	North Bay	707 762-6111 *
Elizabeth Johnson		916 534-3250 *
Steve Butler		916 677-5498
Hal Or Kathy Shore	Sacramento	916 962-0722 *

Dandie Dinmont
Loree Levy		408 266 1221
Betty-Anne Senmark		415 468-2044
Dora Ortwein		707 996-9472

Doberman Pinscher
Darlene Young		408 559-1539
Betty Smith	Monterey	408 625-0366 *
Nancy Heitzon	Monterey	408 659-4202
Valerie Christenson		408 734-5834 *
Cobby Sova, Dpcnc		415 595-1010 *
Anna Browning		415 637-9945
Sharon Messina		510 253-1149
Elizabeth Adjan		510 532-5040
Alan Or Debbe Katz		510 685-9550
Pat Neller		510 825-3215
Joanne Oerlin	Ref	510 837-4508
Karen Lair		707 255-1057
Jolene Ladyman	Club	707 448-3850 *
Brenda Bartholomew		707 762-1152

English Cocker Spaniel
Jean Bobbitt		415 386-2611 *
Charlie Matuk		510 283-6111 *
Barbara Junior		510 528-2490 *
Sandra Close		510 846-9512 *
Karen Ward		510 934-9596

English Setter

Phyliss Williams		408 354-7205	*
Mary Ann Samuelson		408 997-2605	*
Barbara Wood		510 657-4690	*
Juli Jensen	Club	916 689-8346	*

English Springer Spaniel

Valerie Christensen		408 734-5834	
Frieda Rose	South Bay	408 942-3359	*
Diane Tibault	Coordinator	510 482-3199	*

English Toy Spaniel

Loree Levy	408 266-1221
Terri Bullis	415 952-6520

Field Spaniel

No breed rescue known. Contact local or national club.

Finnish Spitz

Wayne Peters	415 325-3947

Flat-Coated Retriever

Ricki Or Peter Gruhl	415 927-9453

Fox Terrier

Nancy Wolf	South Bay	408 438-1159	
Ehren Webster, Ftcnc	Ref	415 329-1719	*
Judy Cullina		415 697-1921	
Linda Cooley		510 443-9838	

Foxhound(American)

Candy Gaiser	Ref	510 487-9783

Foxhound(English)

No breed rescue known. Contact local or national club.

German Shepherd Dog

Barbara Adcock	Ref	408 274-4444	
Janice Raeburn	Ref	510 449-5133	*
Ruby Hertz		510 569-4682	*
Lois Gregor		707 938-3351	*
Gs Dog Club Of Sacramento		916 863-9185	*
Patti Verway	White Gsd Only	510 657-5044	

German Shorthaired Pointer

Laura Hansen		510 235-6792
Silke Auberts	Ref	707 644-8068

Giant Schnauzer

Loree Levy		408 266-1221
Judy Debernardi		408 866-4248
Milly Robertson	Ref	415 591-9918
Sherry Mcdowell		707 527-8098

Dog Owners Guide

Golden Retriever

Crystal Gobel	Monterey	408 336-8910	*
Pam Levin	South Bay	408 354-7350	*
Ardith Osborn	North Bay	415 456-6613	*
Carol Porter	Sf Peninsula	415 593-6433	*
Nor Cal Gr Rescue Hotline		510 262-0597	*
Linda Stephens	East Bay	510 783-0276	*
Barbara Taylor	Napa	707 446-6026	*
Ron Or Linda Giorgi		707 778-8170	
Patty Owen	Upper Nor Cal	916 246-8870	*
Jeanette Summers	Auburn	916 432-0148	*
Carla Cathey	Sacramento	916 688-8737	*

Gordon Setter

Carolyn Gold		415 461-3088	*
Joe Or Margaret Green		510 233-9201	*
Diane Ellis		707 987-9463	
Nancy Thompson	1st Contact	916 989-1633	*

Great Dane

Colleen Leahy	408 267-0788	*
Betty Or Bill Thomas	408 377-6851	*
Julie Haun	510 651-7519	*
Mike Or Marlene Baccala	707 447-Dane	*
Patti Mattera	707 448-0214	*
John Or Janis Robak	707 447-7460	

Great Pyrenees Mountain Dog

Jeff Renwick Or Nancy Jeffery		209 627-0254	
Jeff Glover		408 749-1815	*
Dave Or Judith Depew		415 342-2441	*
Joseph Gilcrist		415 344-5413	*
Jeanne Yturbide		415 922-4378	*
Joyce Grable		510 672-2041	*
Debra Sunderland		510 672-2041	*
Eileen Denning		510 886-9398	*
Laura Prather		707 425-5818	*
Jonni Gonzales		707 448-1115	*
Anna Millee		707 823-0245	*
Catherine De La Cruz	Coord	707 829-1655	*
M'lou Beale		707 937-0136	*
Janet Thearle		916 362-1731	*

Greater Swiss Mountain Dog Dog

Kathy or Maurice Ungar	805 255-1167

Greyhound

Janis Harms	209 227-1797	
Barbara Eineichner	408 847-2867	
Penny Noel	408 847-8054	
Susan Netboy	415 851-7812	
Greyhound Club Of No Cal	510 447-4502	*

138

Sue Tomasello		510 525-1433
Sheila Grant		707 422-1247
Greyhound Pets Of America		800 366-1472
Tamara Wilson		916 739-0121

Harrier

Paul Or Karen Crary		408 629-9269 *

Ibizan Hound

Al Or Mary Crume		209 836-5150
Susan Netboy		415 851-7812
Johanna Bice		707 838-0913

Irish Setter

Marilee Larson		510 351-2966
Leslie Lawrence		510 659-0982
Jessi Chiaudano		707 725-2370
Shirley Farrington		909 780-7333
Irish Setter Club Of Sac		916 421-0788 *

Irish Terrier

Renee Or Walt Bullard		415 661-3774
Mary O'brien		510 521-3246
Diana Martin		707 938-4698

Irish Water Spaniel

Nancy Wiley	1st Contact	415 461-7533
Lorna Pumphrey	2nd Contact	209 476-0411

Irish Wolfhound

Marilyn Shaw	Central Vly	209 754-4182 *
Kathy Jacobsen	South Bay	408 377-2462 *
Lois Thomasson	Monterey	408 484-1668 *
Terry & Robin	East Bay	510 689-9765 *
Agnes Tara-Curtis	North Bay	707 823-4665 *
Arline Stockham	North Bay	707 839-1421 *
Susan Mccombs	N Border	916 357-4185 *
Linda Fairbanks	Sacramento	916 795-1915 *

Italian Greyhound

Camille Bakker		408 866-2482 *
Audrey Sutton		408 867-0989
Barbara Arnold		510 932-3454
Judy Osterhout		707 575-7541

Jack Russell Terrier

Dian Elinor	1st Contact	209 745-2488
Pam Garcia		408 848-1588
Jeanette Rettig		415 851-1159
Susan Mcrae		510 799-7594
Jean Coltrin		707 942-6884 *
Louise Snyder		707 964-3622
Pathy Padilla	Jrtca Rescue	310 547-5478 *

Dog Owners Guide

Japanese Chin
Lucien Collins   408 730-2212
Jackie Collins   510 651-6763
Mary Welsh   916 743-1766

Keeshond
Cindy Snow   408 224-0104 *
Wayne Peters   415 325-3947 *
Linda Ball   510 455-0661 *
Penny Manser   1st Contact   800 286-7728 *
Jane Norton   916 753-3244 *

Kerry Blue Terrier
Jack Or Ann Katona   408 996-0188
Linda Aube   510 655-2786
Bill Or Kathy Stidwell   510 886-7098

Komondor (Hungarian)
Betty Chenolman   213 341-3397
Barbara Stevens   408 475-8854
Bev Calcote   408 722-3670
Catherine De La Cruz   707 729-1655

Kuvasz
John Or Debra Fulkerson   510 256-0643
Vickie Prim   702 673-5742
Valerie Eastman   916 268-9462

Kyi-Leos
Harriett Linn   510 685-4019 *

Labrador Retriever
Gglrc Club Hotline   415 361-0261 *
Jane Borders   707 584-0154

Lakeland Terrier
Bob Bridge   Ref   408 463-0213
Jean Heath   510 846-1326

Lhasa Apso
Pat Keen   Central Vly   209 369-4388
Ellen Prior   408 227-CARE
Loree Levy   408 266-1221
Kathy Larue   Ref   707 463-1248

Maltese
Lois Gregg   Ref   209 239-7089
Ellen Prior   408 227-CARE
Loree Levy   408 266-1221
Louise Bialek   916 395-6449

Manchester Terrier, Standard
Pearl Koch   510 934-0915
Dave Or Melodye Elichia   916 622-2232
Shirleen Reeves   916 969-9994
Fred Or Myrtle Klensch   916 652-6998 *

Manchaster Terrier, Toy
Loree Levy	408 266-1221
Fred Or Shirley Carnett	916 622-4149
Myrtle Clinch	916 652-6998

Mastiff
Ellen Prior	408 227-Care *
Dorothy Berney	408 779-3052
Dee Gensburger	707 763-8443
Joanne Williams	707 778-1828
Fred Carnett	916 622-4149 *

Mexican Hairless
Alan Segal	408 663-3235

Miniature Bull Terrier
No breed rescue known. Contact local or national club.

Miniature Pinscher
Alan Segal	408 663-3235
Terri Bullis	415 952-6520
Shawn Brown	916 878-0269

Miniature Schnauzer
Larry Or Georgia Drivon	209 931-5671 *
Margaret Doty	408 736-1293 *
Milly Robertson	415 591-9918 *
Joan Wieder	415 924-9787 *
Glendora Norwood	707 762-5898 *
Beverly Pfaff	707 864-0606 *
Cheryl Mazzoncini	916 724-3218 *

Newfoundland
Joe Ovalle		209 575-4214 *
Lori Littleford	Coordinator	408 286-1855 *
Bari Halperin		415 364-7637 *
Gaby Cohen		415 366-5641 *
Larry Lerner		415 851-0137
Dave Or Kate Anderson		707 528-1346 *
Nancy Bynes	Coordinator	916 265-0525 *

Norfolk Terrier
Neil Hamilton	408 225-8397
Isabel Blumberg	415 854-2170
Linda Ball	510 455-0661
Ed & Ann Dum	510 462-7776
Robin Ormiston	707 446-1722

Norwegian Elkhound
Karen Allen	Ref	415 591-8056
Michelle Fain		707 795-6546
Carl Or Rita Burson		916 791-7042 *
Ken Or Judy Strakein		916 967-3237

Dog Owners Guide

Norwich Terrier
Niel Hamilton		408 225-8397
Isabel Blumberg		415 854-2170
Linda Ball		510 455-0661

Old English Sheepdog
Regina Wallen		408 926-1226	
Mary Skelton		415 365-9938	
Pam Henry		707 579-1848	*
Margaret Welty		916 677-7707	
Florence Or Lowell Narron		510 846-0401	*
Famous Or Margie Holt		707 792-2395	*
Salle Jantz	Sac Only	916 446-7405	*
Karen Or Fred Stetler		916 695-3500	*
Patrick Butler		916 969-4366	

Otterhound
No breed rescue known. Contact local or national club.

Papillon
Loree Levy		408 266-1221	
Pearl George	Ref	408 353-1496	
Rosalie Palmer	Bay Area Only	415 323-7997	
Annabelle Hofmann		805 964-2446	*
Don Or Jeri Mcgill		916 666-3916	*

Pekingese
Loree Levy		408 266-1221	
Patti Hempel	South Bay	408 377-7718	*
Frieda Rose	South Bay	408 942-3359	
Lorraine Morton		510 223-0633	*
Florence Mccauley	Ref	707 446-7353	
Breana Bartholomew		707 762-1152	

Petits Bassets Griffons Vendee
No breed rescue known. Contact local or national club.

Pharoah Hound
Susan Netboy		415 851-7812
Dom Delmore	1st Contact	415 865-9418
Sandra Wornum		415 924-7020
Sue Seffcik		916 687-6696

Pomeranian
Ellen Prior		408 227-Care
Loree Levy		408 266-1221
Marge Kranzelder	Ref	415 572-0149

Poodle ,Miniature
Ellen Prior		408 227-Care	
Joanne Finch		415 369-8970	
Marge Kranzelder		415 572-0149	
Norcal Poodle Rescue		510 295-1070	
Roberta Stone		415 892-3191	*
Ingeborg Sesenschin		707 425-5005	*

Poodle, Standard

Norcal Poodle Rescue		510 295-0353
Betty Janz	Grass Vly	916 273-7943
Florence Graham		415 479-4229 *

Poodle, Toy

Norcal Poodle Rescue		510 295-0353
Roberta Stone		415 892-3191 *

Portuguese Water Dog

Janet Mekeel	209 576-1910 *
Cheryl Smith	408 358-2136 *
Judy Archambeau	707 539-6465 *
Becky Morin	916 987-0537 *

Pug

Nancy Ford	408 252-0598
Sue Natoli	415 592-0732
Donna Manha	510 793-8276
Breana Bartholomew	707 762-1152
Anne Fairchild	916 722-1227

Puli

Barbara Or Nancy	408 354-0726 *
Jerry Motter	408 728-4641
Julius Or Terry Hidassy	408 736-0786
Frank Washburn	415 349-6853

Rhodesian Ridgeback

Betty Scattini	Ref	408 484-1433
Linda Batson	South Bay Only	408 688-7001
Elizabeth Akers		510 825-9258
Diane Jacobsen		707 829-0768

Rottweiler

Rose Fullen		209 584-6714
Carrie Schmidt		408 353-1441
Kathy Stanley	1st Contact	408 763-1257 *
Dee Hernandez	S Bay/Montarey	408 848-3368
Jill Kessler		408 726-1130 *
Linda Lopez		510 235-9553 *
Joanne Or Rick Marino		510 733-2374
Doris Baldwin	Ref	510 945-1509 *
Gavin Slabbert		916 652-7687 *
Susan Hildebrand	Club	916 756-8633 *

Saluki

Sharon Kincaid	408 246-5346
Susan Netboy	415 851-7812
Sandra Wornum	415 924-7020
Sheila Grant	707 422-1247

Samoyed

Ellen Prior		408 227-Care
Nick Matulich		408 379-7253
Barbara Or Norm Weinstein		415 851-0648
Wilma Coulter	Club Rescue	415 593-2281 *
Pat Enslen	Club Rescue	415 583-6844 *

Schipperke

Cathy Montgomery		408 779-9257
Barbara Guerina		408 848-1296
Shirley Emmons		707 224-4192 *
Sue Johnson		805 722-1797

Scottish Deerhound

Allyn Brewer-Babbitch	408 251-6788
Peggy Kopf	408 257-0103
Valery Howes	415 726-5778
Susan Netboy	415 851-7812
Cheryl Roberts	510 237-0433
Noel Or Liz Kennedy	707 585-8133
Frieda Pilat	805 251-3516

Scottish Terrier

Mike Serrano	Sacramento	209 748-2277 *
Bill Or Peggy Burge	South Bay	408 238-2327 *
Danny Graves	Coordinator	408 453-6483 *
Ed Or Benja Nicholas	S Bay	408 662-0970 *
Debbie Knous	Sf Peninsula	415 345-0245 *
Lynn Huffaker	North Bay	415 892-9501 *
Don Or Pat Siegel	Sacramento	916 758-5140 *

Sealyham Terrier

Debbie Knous	415 345-0245

Shar-Pei (Chinese)

Carol Cretser		209 575-1717
Diane Gil	Coordinator	408 225-7787
Liz Montgomery		510 373-1939
Bertha Martin		510 634-3144 *
Dawn Walling		510 862-2228
Sacramento Club Rescue		916 991-0223 *

Shetland Sheepdog

Amy Bradstad	408 274-3830 *
Marianne Dub	408 297-0762 *
Helen Laycock	408 438-5507 *
Diane Bassett	415 359-5181 *
Loretta Dillinger	510 254-8353
Pam Ferguson	510 527-1643
Kathy Lovig	510 778-7130
Pat Mahoney	510 846-0340 *
Charles Or Jan Warziniack	707 527-8115 *
Tami Collier	916 362-8870 *

Shiba Inu
Dorothy Warren   408 867-2467

Shih Tzu
Loree Levy   408 266-1221
Kathy Larue   Ref   707 463-1248

Siberian Husky
Shila Kuesthardt   Ref   209 524-7631 *
Nancy   Shelter Emgy Only   209 835-7445
Nick Matulich   408 379-7253
Linda Mullen   Santa Cruz Only   408 426-2151 *
Gloria Or Sandy Senteney   415 595-5856
Barbara/Norm Weinstein   Eves   415 851-0648
Marilyn Lassagne   Club   510 820-1162 *
Laura Brotman   707 762-6511

Silky Terrier
Loree Levy   408 266-1221
Louise Bialek   916 395-6449

Skye Terrier
Carol Simmonds   415 897-1144
Judy Davis   916 674-2682

Soft-Coated Wheaten Terrier
Elaine Or Bob Nerrie   415 327-4830
Robyn Alexander   510 526-7948

St. Bernard
Jill Urbina   Ref   408 377-0431 *
John Or Martha Laden   Ref   510 657-0645
Penny Mahan   707 996-4319 *
Styron Pool   Central Vly   916 885-6304 *

Staffordshire Bull Terrier
No breed rescue known. Contact local or national club.

Standard Schnauzer
Shirley Rude   415 435-3034

Sussex Spaniel
No breed rescue known. Contact local or national club.

Tibetan Spaniel
John & Angelee Fargo   707 795-9103

Tibetan Terrier
Robert Or Dorothy Chase   408 423-3755
Bonnie Schlein   415 851-5155
Anne Keleman   415 897-7431 *
Jeanette Or Jerry Chaix   707 887-7616 *

Vizsla (Hungarian)
Sandy Parady   408 338-3657 *
Steve Shlyen   415 566-9289 *

Weimaraner
Kathy Dunn		415 635-3821 *
Debra Hopkins		916 723-7340 *

Welsh Springer Spaniel
Shelly Monson		415 648-7848

Welsh Terrier
Kent Or Lurlene Williams		209 523-1778 *
Deborah Jamison	Coordinator	408 725-0424 *
Jean Heath		510 846-1326 *
Mary Smith		707 823-2051 *
Karen Or Rc Williams		916 677-4815 *

West Highland White Terrier
Marge Conway		209 297-0845
Pam Or Diane	1st Contact	408 274-8718 *
Jo Dodson Raleigh		510 524-1942
George Or Sharon Fry		707 778-0333
Toni Snow		916 961-3692

Whippet
Carolyn Simpson		209 523-8539 *
Debbie Sparks		408 247-1749 *
Judith Benson		415 342-8868 *
Carol Gregory	Coordinator	510 736-7340 *
Kathy Graves		707 527-4072

Wirehaired Pointing Griffon
No breed rescue known. Contact local or national club.

Yorkshire Terrier
Virginia Denton	Sac Only	209 726-9147 *
Loree Levy		408 266-1221
Kay Stangeland	Eves	415 446-2008 *
Isabel Blumberg		415 854-2170

Appendix C
Breed Cautions

This section is designed to offer the most serious and most common warnings prevalent in the breed. Buying from a quality breeder who offers certification will help reduce the likelihood of having to spend large sums of money on treatment, but remember, no breeder can be 100% sure.

Hip Dysplasia   An inherited problem where the hip does not fit properly into the socket. The best prevention is to X-ray the parents. X-rays are not 100% foolproof, but they decrease the odds immensely.

Progressive Retinal Atrophy (PRA)   This inherited disease results in severe loss of vision and usually blindness. The best prevention is buying only puppies whose parents' eyes were examined by a canine ophthalmologist and found to be free of hereditary eye conditions before being bred. Usually the breeder sends the tests to the Canine Eye Registry Foundation (CERF) for evaluation and an official clearance certificate. If a breed is listed as having PRA or hereditary cataracts, ask to see the CERF certificates or a letter from a canine ophthalmologist.

von Willebrand's Disease   This is a blood-clotting disorder of genetic origin and produces external or internal hemorrhaging from a simple cut or illness. The best prevention is to buy only from parents whose blood was tested and found free of the condition before being bred.

Bloat
This condition strikes large, deep chested breeds. The stomach swells with food, water or internal gases, seals itself off from relief, and may suddenly twist or flip over, resulting in death, unless there is surgical intervention. Feed small meals at least one to two hours after exercise.

Slipped Stifle
This is a joint disorder.

List of Cautions by Breed. The name of the breed is printed in **bold type**, followed by the caution in plain type.

NOTE: All dogs listed below are good with children except as noted.

Affenpinscher: Susceptible to slipped stifle. Poor interaction with children.

Afghan Hound: Susceptible to hip dysplasia. Many breeders do not check hips because it requires anesthesia and the breed is sensitive to drugs. Needs extensive grooming, exercise. Poor interaction with children. Apartment not recommended.

Airedale Terrier: Susceptible to hip dysplasia. Buy only from OFA registered parents. Needs exercise. Tolerant with children.

Akita (Japanese): Susceptible to hip dysplasia and PRA. Buy only from OFA and CERF registered parents. Tolerant with children.

Alaskan Malamute: Susceptible to hip dysplasia, Does not like heat with his thick coat. Buy from OFA registered parents. Needs lots of exercise. Apartment not recommended.

American Eskimo: This breed has no real health problems and is considered a long-lived breed.

American Staffordshire Terrier: Susceptible to hip dysplasia. Buy only from OFA registered parents. Needs lots of exercise. Need caution around children.

American Water Spaniel: Susceptible to hip dysplasia. Buy only from OFA registered parents. Needs lots of exercise. Not good around children.

Australian Cattle Dog: Susceptible to hip dysplasia. Buy from OFA registered parents. Needs lots of exercise. Good with older children. Apartment not recommended.

Australian Shepherd: Hip dysplasia, buy only from OFA registered breeders, also Collie Eye Anomaly is present in some. Needs lots of exercise. Apartment not recommended.

Australian Terrier: Healthy breed, prone to no real problems. Tolerant of children.

Basenji: Comes in heat once a year. Tolerant with children. Fanconi Syndrome (kidney problem). Susceptible to PRA. Buy only from CERF registered parents.

Basset Hound: Susceptible to bloat. Buying from poor breeder can result in ill tempered, sickly dog.

Beagle: Susceptible to bloat. Poor breeding can result in ill-tempered, sickly dog. Needs lots of exercise.

Bearded Collie: Susceptible to hip dysplasia, epilepsy. Buy only from OFA registered parents. Apartment not recommended.

Bedlington Terrier: Susceptible to PRA. Tolerant with children.

Belgian Malinois: Susceptible to hip dysplasia. Buy only from OFA registered parents. Extensive grooming. Needs lots of exercise. Apartment not recommended.

Belgian Sheepdog: Susceptible to hip dysplasia. Buy only from OFA registered parents. Extensive grooming. Needs lots of exercise. OK with older children. Apartment not recommended.

Belgian Tervuren: Susceptible to hip dysplasia. Buy only from OFA registered parents. Extensive grooming. Needs lots of exercise. Apartment not recommended.

Bernese Mtn Dog: Short lived breed (10 Yrs.), Susceptible to hip and elbow dysplasia, bloat and some eye problems. With thick coat, does not like heat. Buy only from OFA registered parents (hips and elbows). Needs extensive grooming. Apartment not recommended.

Bichon Frise: Kartagener's disease, canine bladder stones, skin conditions. Needs regular grooming. may be hard to housebreak, not outside dogs.

Black and Tan Coonhound: Susceptible to hip dysplasia. Avoid field types if you want a household pet. Needs lots of exercise. Apartment not recommended.

Bloodhound: Short lived breed (10 yrs). Susceptible to hip dysplasia and bloat. Buy only from OFA registered parents. Needs lots of exercise. Apartment not recommended.

Border Collies: Susceptible to hip dysplasia and PRA. Buy only from OFA, CERF registered parents. Needs lots of exercise. Apartment not recommended.

Border Terrier: Susceptible to hip dysplasia. Buy only from OFA registered parents.

Borzoi: Susceptible to bloat. Sensitive to drugs. Needs extensive grooming. Poor interaction with children. Apartment not recommended.

Boston Terrier: Susceptible to infections and lacerations on protruding eyes, also respiratory difficulties and heatstroke because of his pushed-in-face. Avoid hot, stuffy conditions and closed cars. Protect from extremes of temperature.

Bouvier des Flandres: Susceptible to hip dysplasia and bloat. Buy only from OFA registered parents. Needs lots of exercise. Apartment not recommended.

Boxer: Short lived breed (10 Yrs.), susceptible to hip dysplasia and bloat. Sensitive to hot, stuffy weather, heatstroke. Careful of enclosed cars. Buy from OFA registered parents.

Briard: Susceptible to hip dysplasia, PRA, and bloat. Buy only from OFA and CERF registered parents. Apartment not recommended.

Brittany: Susceptible to hip dysplasia. Buy only from OFA registered owners. Needs lots of exercise.

Brussels Griffon: Susceptible to heatstroke and slipped stifle. Tolerant with children.

Bull Terrier: Susceptible to skin problems. Tolerant with children.

Bulldog: Shortlived breed (10 yrs). Hereditary throat problems, heat stroke, entropia, sensitive to anesthesia.

Bullmastiff: Short-lived breed, susceptible to hip dysplasia, bloat and eyelid problems. Buy only from OFA registered parents. Needs lots of exercise. Apartment not recommended.

Cairn Terrier: Susceptible to skin allergies. Tolerant with children.

Cavalier King Charles Spaniel: Susceptible to slipped stifle. Needs extensive grooming.

Chesapeake Bay Retriever: Susceptible to hip dysplasia and PRA. Buy only from OFA and CERF registered parents. Needs lots of exercise.

Chihuahua: Long lived breed (15 yrs), susceptible to slipped stifle. Poor interaction with children.

Chow Chow: Susceptible to hip dysplasia. Buy only from OFA registered parents. Does not like heat. Needs extensive grooming. Poor interaction with children.

Clumber Spaniel: Susceptible to hip dysplasia. Buy only from OFA registered parents. Needs lots of exercise.

Cocker Spaniel: Susceptible to hip dysplasia and PRA. Buy only from OFA, CERF registered parents. Needs extensive grooming. Needs lots of exercise.

Collie: Susceptible to PRA and CEA (Collie Eye Anomaly), Buy only from CERF registered parents. The Roughs need extensive grooming. Needs lots of exercise.

Curly-Coated Retriever: Susceptible to hip dysplasia and PRA. Buy only from OFA and CERF registered parents. Needs lots of exercise.

Dachshund: Long lived breed (15 yrs.) Susceptible to spinal disc problems. Miniatures have poor interaction with young children. Don't overfeed.

Dalmatian: Some puppies are born deaf or can only hear out of one ear. Buy only from OFA registered parents. Best breeders B.A.E.R. test puppies for hearing. Needs lots of exercise. Sheds a lot. Apartment not recommended.

Dandie Dinmont: Susceptible to spinal disc problems. Don't let him jump off high furniture. Poor interaction with children.

Doberman Pinscher: Susceptible to hip dysplasia, von Willebrand's disease, bloat. Buy only from OFA registered, VWD tested parents. Need lots of exercise. Tolerant with children. Happiest with family indoors. Protect from extremes in temperature.

English Cocker Spaniel: Susceptible to hip dysplasia and PRA. Buy only from OFA, CERF registered parents.

English Setter: Susceptible to hip dysplasia. Buy only from OFA registered parents. Needs lots of exercise. Apartment not recommended.

English Springer Spaniel: Susceptible to hip dysplasia and PRA. Buy only from OFA and CERF registered parents. Needs lots of exercise.

English Toy Spaniel : Susceptible to slipped stifle and heatstroke. Needs extensive grooming.

Field Spaniel: Susceptible to hip dysplasia. Buy only from OFA registered parents. Needs lots of exercise. Apartment not recommended.

Finnish Spitz: Susceptible to hip dysplasia and PRA. Buy only from OFA, CERF registered parents. Needs lots of exercise.

Flat-Coated Retriever: Susceptible to hip dysplasia and PRA. Buy only from OFA and CERF registered parents. Needs lots of exercise.

Fox Terrier, Smooth: Long lived breed (15 yrs.) Susceptible to deafness.

Fox Terrier, Wire: Long lived breed (15 yrs.) Susceptible to deafness.

Foxhound, American: Healthy breed, no real problems. Needs lots of exercise. Apartment not recommended.

Foxhound, English: Healthy breed, no real problems. Needs lots of exercise. Apartment not recommended.

French Bulldog: Susceptible to lacerations on eyes, respiratory difficulties and heatstroke. Protect from extreme heat, avoid enclosed cars. Large percentage of this breed die of carcinoma. Sensitive to anesthesia. Poor interaction with children.

German Shepherd: Susceptible to hip dysplasia and bloat. Buy only from OFA registered parents. Most frequent problem is personality and temperament. Buy only from reputable breeder. Needs lots of exercise.

German Shorthaired Pointer: Susceptible to hip dysplasia. Buy only from OFA registered parents. Needs lots of exercise. Poor interaction with children. Apartment not recommended.

German Wirehaired Pointer: Susceptible to hip dysplasia. Buy only from OFA registered parents. Needs lots of exercise. Poor interaction with children. Apartment not recommended.

Giant Schnauzer: Susceptible to hip dysplasi. Buy only from OFA registered parents. Needs lots of exercise. Poor interaction with children. Apartment not recommended.

Golden Retriever: Susceptible to hip dysplasia, PRA and von Willebrand's disease. Buy only from OFA and CERF registered parents. Needs extensive grooming. Needs lots of exercise.

Gordon Setter: Susceptible to hip dysplasia. Buy only from OFA registered parents. Needs lots of exercise. Apartment not recommended.

Great Dane: Short lived breed (10 yrs.), susceptible to hip dysplasia and bloat. Buy only from OFA registered parents. Low tolerance to tranquilizers. Apartment not recommended.

Great Pyrenees: Short lived breed (10 yrs.), susceptible to hip dysplasia and bloat. Buy only from OFA registered parents. Apartment not recommended.

Greyhound: Susceptible to bloat. Sensitive to drugs. Needs lots of exercise. OK in apartments.

Harrier: Healthy breed with no real problems. Needs lots of exercise. Apartment not recommended.

Ibizan Hound: Sensitive to drugs. Some hip dysplasia. Needs lots of exercise.

Irish Setter: Susceptible to hip dysplasia, PRA and bloat. Buy only from OFA and CERF registered parents. Needs extensive grooming. Needs lots of exercise. Apartment not recommended.

Irish Terrier: Healthy breed, prone to no real problems.

Irish Water Spaniel: Susceptible to hip dysplasia.. Buy only from OFA registered parents. Needs lots of exercise, extensive grooming. Poor interaction with children. Apartment not recommended.

Irish Wolfhound: Short lived breed (8-10 yrs) Susceptible to hip dysplasia and bloat. Buy only from OFA registered parents. Extensive grooming. Apartment not recommended.

Italian Greyhound: Susceptible to slipped stifle. Poor interaction with children.

Jack Russell Terrier: Susceptible to a congenital dwarfism, where a puppy has a normal head and body but short legs. Apartment not recommended.

Japanese Chin: Susceptible to lacerations on eyes and heatstroke — avoid hot, stuffy conditions and cold and damp.

Keeshond: Susceptible to hip dysplasia. He does not like the heat. Needs extensive grooming.

Kerry Blue Terrier: Long-lived breed (15 yrs.) Susceptible to hip dysplasia. Buy only from OFA registered parents. Needs lots of exercise. Poor interaction with children.

Komondor: Susceptible to hip dysplasia and bloat. Buy only from OFA registered parents. Extensive grooming. Poor interaction with children. Apartment not recommended.

Kuvasz: Short lived breed (10yrs). Susceptible to hip dysplasia and bloat. Buy only from OFA registered parents. Needs lots of exercise. Poor interaction with children. Apartment not recommended.

Labrador Retriever: Susceptible to hip dysplasia, PRA, and bloat. Buy only from OFA and CERF registered parents.

Lakeland Terrier: Healthy breed, prone to no real problems.

Lhasa Apso: Susceptible to hip dysplasia. Buy only from OFA registered parents. Needs extensive grooming. Poor interaction with children.

Maltese: Susceptible to slipped stifle (a joint disorder). Needs extensive grooming. Poor interaction with children.

Manchester, Standard: Susceptible to bleeding disorders. Poor interaction with children.

Manchester, Toy: Susceptible to slipped stifle. Poor interaction with children.

Mastiff: Short-lived breed (10 yrs.), susceptible to hip dysplasia. Buy only from OFA registered parents. Apartment not recommended.

Miniature Pinscher: Prone to demodectic mange under stress. Poor interaction with children.

Miniature Schnauzer: Susceptible to cataracts and skin conditions. Extensive grooming.

Newfoundland: Short lived breed (10 years). Susceptible to hip dysplasia. Buy only from OFA registered parents. Needs extensive grooming. Apartment not recommended.

Norfolk Terrier: Healthy breed, prone to no real problems.

Norwegian Elkhound: Susceptible to hip dysplasia. Buy only from OFA registered parents. Poor interaction with children.

Norwich Terrier: Healthy breed, prone to no real problems.

Old English Sheepdog: Susceptible to hip dysplasia and PRA. Buy only from OFA, CERF registered parents. Needs extensive grooming. Apartment not recommended.

Otterhound: Susceptible to hip dysplasia and bloat. Buy only from OFA registered parents. Needs lots of exercise. Apartment not recommended.

Papillon: Susceptible to slipped stifle. Needs extensive grooming. Poor interaction with children.

Pekingese: Susceptible to eye problems, respiratory difficulties and heatstroke. Needs extensive grooming. Poor interaction with children.

Pharoah Hound: Sensitive to drugs. Needs lots of exercise. Apartment not recommended.

Pomeranian: Susceptible to slipped stifle. Needs extensive grooming. Poor interaction with children.

Poodle, Miniature: Susceptible to hip dysplasia, PRA. Buy from OFA, CERF registered parents. Needs extensive grooming.

Poodle,Standard: Susceptible to hip dysplasia, PRA, von Willebrand's Disease and bloat. Buy only from OFA and CERF registered and VWD tested parents. Needs extensive grooming. Needs exercise. Inside dogs.

Poodle, Toy: Susceptible to hip dysplasia and PRA. Buy only from OFA, CERF registered parents. Needs extensive grooming. Poor interaction with children.

Portuguese Water Dog: Susceptible to hip dysplasia and PRA. Buy only from OFA and CERF registered parents. Needs lots of exercise.

Pug: Susceptible to eye problems and heatstroke. Avoid hot stuffy conditions. Sensitive to anesthesia.

Puli: Susceptible to hip dysplasia. Buy only from OFA registered parents. Needs lots of exercise. Extensive grooming. Poor interaction with children.

Rhodesian Ridgeback: Susceptible to hip dysplasia. Buy only from OFA registered parents. Needs lots of exercise.

Rottweiler: Susceptible to hip dysplasia, elbow dysplasia and bloat. Buy only from OFA registered parents. Needs lots of exercise. Caution around children. Insurance in effect? Apartment not recommended.

Saluki: Susceptible to some hip dysplasia. Needs lots of exercise. Poor interaction with children. Apartment not recommended.

Samoyed: Susceptible to hip dysplasia and PRA. Buy only from OFA and CERF registered parents. Needs lots of attention. Requires regular brushings. Tendency to bark if left alone.

Schipperke: Long lived breed (15 years). Prone to no real problems

Scottish Deerhound: Short lived breed (10 yrs.) Susceptible to bloat. Needs lots of exercise.

155

Scottish Terrier: Susceptible to von Willebrand's disease, scotty cramp (minor discomfort walking). Needs extensive grooming. Apartment not recommended.

Sealyham Terrier: Long-lived breed (15 years). Susceptible to skin conditions.

Shar-Pei (Chinese): Short lived breed (10 yrs). Susceptible to hip dysplasia, skin problems and entropion. Buy only from OFA registered parents. Poor interaction with children.

Shetland Sheepdog: Susceptible to hip dysplasia, PRA, CEA (Collie Eye Anomaly). Buy only from OFA, CERF registered parents.

Shiba Inu: They are susceptible to hip dysplasia and PRA. Buy only from OFA and CERF registered parents.

Shih Tzu: Kidney problems. Needs extensive grooming.

Siberian Husky: Susceptible to some hip dysplasia, PRA, Buy only from OFA and CERF registered parents. Needs lots of exercise.

Silky Terrier: Healthy breed, no real problems. Extensive grooming.

Skye Terrier: Healthy breed, prone to no real problems. Needs extensive grooming.

Soft Coated Wheaten: Susceptible to PRA. Buy only from CERF registered parents. Needs lots of exercise. Extensive grooming.

St. Bernard: Short lived breed (10yrs.), Susceptible to hip dysplasia and bloat. Buy only from OFA registered parents. Needs extensive grooming. Apartment not recommended.

Staffordshire Bull Terrier: Susceptible to hip dysplasia. Buy only from OFA Registered breeder. Needs lots of exercise. Poor interaction with children.

Standard Pointer: Susceptible to hip dysplasia. Buy only from OFA registered parents. Needs lots of exercise.

Standard Schnauzer: A long-lived breed (15yrs.), susceptible to hip dysplasia. Buy only from OFA registered parents. Needs lots of exercise. Extensive grooming. Poor interaction with children.

Tibetan Spaniel: Healthy breed, prone to no real problems.

Tibetan Terrier: Susceptible to hip dysplasia and PRA. Buy only from OFA and CERF registered parents. Poor interaction with children.

Vizsla: Susceptible to hip dysplasia. Buy only from OFA registered parents. Needs lots of exercise. Apartment not recommended.

Weimaraner: Susceptible to hip dysplasia and bloat. Buy only from OFA registered parents. Needs lots of exercise. Apartment not recommended.

Welsh Corgi, Cardigan: Susceptible to hip dysplasia and PRA. Buy only from OFA and CERF registered parents.

Welsh Corgi, Pembroke : Susceptible to hip dysplasia and PRA. Buy only from OFA and CERF registered parents. ;

Welsh Springer Spaniel: Susceptible to hip dysplasia and PRA. Buy only from OFA and CERF registered parents. Needs lots of exercise.

Welsh Terrier: No apparent health problems

West Highland White Terrier: Long-lived breed (15 yrs.) Susceptible to skin conditions. Needs extensive grooming.

Whippet: Sensitive to drugs. Sensitive emotionally. Should be protected from cold. Needs lots of exercise. Poor interaction with children.

Wirehaired Pointing Griffon: Susceptible to hip dysplasia. Buy only from OFA registered parents. Needs lots of exercise. Poor interaction with children. Apartment not recommended.

Yorkshire Terrier: Susceptible to slipped stifle. Needs extensive grooming. Poor interaction with children.

Appendix D
Service Directory

The following list of service providers is offered as an aid to the public in finding dog-related services. *Northern California Dog Owners Guide* does not recommend, guarantee, endorse, nor rate service providers. We do not assume any liability.

Acupuncturist, Canine

There is growing interest in the use of acupuncture in the treatment of animals.

International Veterinary
Acupuncture Society
2140 Conestoga Rd.
Chester Springs, PA 19425
215 827-7245

Adoption Service for Seniors

Pets for People
1 800 345-5678

SF SPCA
415 554-3000 (Free Adoption)

Humane Society of Santa Clara Vly
Senior Pets For Senior

Agility Clubs

U S Dog Agility Assoc.
P O Box 850955
Richardson, TX 75085
214 231-9700

National Agility Club
401 Bluemont Circle
Manhattan, KS 66502
913 537-7022

Haute Dawgs Agility Group
800 770-7166

Susan Anderson
916 678-8703

Pamela Hartley
408 982-0228

Karen TenEyck
408 370-7213

County Wide Dog Training Club
707 823-0379

National Club for Dog Agility
Virginia Isaac
916 966-5287

Foothill Dog Training Agility
408 729-6983

San Francisco Agility

AIDS/HIV Assistance

Pets Are Wonderful
415 241-1460

All-Breed Clubs in Northern California

Sacramento Council of Dog Clubs
916 483-3602

Golden State Kennel Club (UKC)
Jacki Root
916 967-5576

Salinas Valley Kennel Club
1455 Marin Ave
SalinasCA93906
Diana Smith
408 449-5339

Del Monte Kennel Club
PO Box 22461
CarmelCA93922
Mrs Mary Carpenter
408 624-4429

Santa Clara Valley Kennel Club
2380 Santa Ana
Palo Alto, CA 94303
Rita Perko
415 858-1111

Del Valle Dog Club of Livermore
927 Aberdeen Ave
Livermore, CA 94550
C Ann Burton
510 447-5553

Contra Costa County Kennel Club
63949 Canyon Place
Lafayette, CA 94549
Victoria Cochran
510 284-1882

Golden Gate Kennel Club
47 San Pablo Court
Moraga, CA 94556
Helen A Hanson
510 631-1466

Wine Country Kennel Club
4001 Middle Rd
Napa, CA 94559
Martha Fiedler
707 252-1404

San Mateo Kennel Club
9601 Broadmoor Drive
San Ramon, CA 94583
Mrs. Patricia Johnson
510 828-5143

Oakland Kennel Club
5400 Proctor Ave
Oakland, CA 94618
Mr Maurice Ferrero
510 339-2375

Sir Francis Drake Kennel Club
PO Box 62
Corte Madera, CA 94976
Donald Lawler
415 924-6585

Santa Cruz Kennel Club
3851 Branciforte Dr
Santa Cruz, CA 95060
Pamela Gangloff
408 426-8094

Coyote Hills Kennel Club
514350 Skyline Blvd
Oakland, CA 94629
Ruby Hertz
510 635-4540

Richmond Dog Fanciers Club
1170 Roberts Ave
San Jose, CA 95122
Mrs Ruth Davidson
408 947-7812

Redwood Empire Kennel Club
1130 Butler Ave
Santa Rosa, CA 95407
Thomas Tracy
707 546-8763

Mensona Kennel Club
5860 Gilmore Ave
Cotati, CA 94931
Michele Fain
707 795-6546

Shasta Kennel Club
11531 Bonnie Brae Ln
Redding, CA 96003
Marge Sparks
916 549-5219

Chief Solano Kennel Club
160 Randall Ave
Vacaville, CA 95687
Sheri Hubbell
707 447-6877

Chico Dog Fanciers Assoc
P O Box 1096
Durham, CA 95938
Lynda Piercy
916 343-5171

Sacramento Kennel Club
1031 El Sur Way
Sacramento, CA 95825
Rosemarie Blood
916 972-8559

Sacramento Valley Dog Fanciers
27701 Robben Rd
Dixon, CA 95620
Ellen Haro
916 972-8559

Two Cities Kennel Club
6938 S George Washington
Yuba City, CA 95993
Beverly Millette
916 673-1925

Donner Trail Kennel Club
4231 Bannister Rd
Fair Oaks, CA 95628
Judy Strakbein
916 967-3237

Sierra-Tuolomne Kennel Club
14801 Lakeside Dr
Sonora, CA 95370
Sherry Galka
209 532-9217

Animal Abuse Hotline

Call your local humane society or SPCA

Dog Owners Guide

Animal Agent for Film, TV & Ads

Brian McMillan's Animal Rentals
31305 Tick Canyon Rd
Canyon Country, CA 91351

Julie Sandoval Stubbings
805 252-4509

Animal Shelters by County (see also Humane Societies)

Animal shelters are responsible for adoptions, as well as, enforcement of animal laws, investigation of violations and initiation of prosecution as required, dog licensing, Rabies prevention programs, control of vicious dogs, spay/neuter referral programs, public education, owner notification of found, licensed dogs, kennel licensing and inspection and humane disposal of old, injured or unwanted animals.

Santa Clara County

Palo Alto Animal Services
3281 E Bayshore
Palo Alto, CA 94303
408 329-2671

Watsonville Animal Shelter
PO Box 1930
Watsonville, CA 95077
408 722-0622

Santa Clara Animal Shelter
12370 Murphy Ave
San Martin, CA 95046
408 683-4186

San Francisco County

SF Animal Care & Control
1200 15th St
San Francisco, CA 94103
415 554-6364

Marin County

St Francis Animal Protection
PO Box 214
Corte Madera, CA 94976
707 435-2097

Napa County

Napa County Animal Control
942 W Imola Place
Napa, CA 94559
707 253-4381

162

Appendix D: Service Directory

Solano County

Solano County Animal Control
2510 Claybank Rd
Fairfield, CA 94533
707 421-7486

Sonoma County

Healdsburg Animal Shelter
570 Westside Rd
Healdsburg, CA 95448
707 431-3386

Pets Life Line
PO Box 341
Sonoma, CA 95476
707 996-4577

Rohnert Park Animal Shelter
5663 Redwood Dr
Rohnert Park, CA
707 584-1582

Petaluma City Animal Shelter
840 Hopper St
Petaluma, CA 94952
707 778-4396

Alemeda County

Alameda County Animal Control
2700 Fairmont Dr
San Leandro, CA 94577
510 667-7707

Santa Rita Animal Shelter
4051 Altamirano
Pleasanton, CA 94566
510 828-0824

Tri City Animal Shelter
1950 Stevenson Blvd
Fremont, CA 94538
510 790-6777

Livermore City Shelter
1050 S Livermore Ave
Livermore, CA 94550
510 373-5303

Oakland Animal Shelter
3065 Ford St
Oakland, CA
510 238-3563

Berkeley Animal Shelter
2013 2nd St
Berkeley, CA 94710
510 644-6755

Alemeda City Animal Shelter
1590 Fortmann Way
Alameda, CA 94501
510 522-4100

Union City Animal Control
34009 Alvarado Niles Rd
Union City, CA 94587
510 471-1365

Alameda City Animal Shelter
2043 Grand St
Alameda, CA 94501
510 828-0824

Hayward Animal Shelter
16 Barnes Ct
Hayward, CA
510 537-7560

Dog Owners Guide

Contra Costa County

Martinez Animal Shelter
4849 Imhoff Place
Martinez, CA
510 646-2995

Antioch City Shelter
300 L St
Antioch, CA 94509
510 757-2278

Pinole Animal Shelter
651 Pinole Shores Dr
Pinole, CA 94564
510 374-3966

Sacramento County

Sacramento City Animal Control
2127 Front St
Sacramento, CA 95818
916 264-7387

Sacramento Co Animal Control
4290 Bradshaw
Sacramento, CA 95815
916 336-2632

San Joaquin County

San Joaquin Co Animal Control
1686 E Hazelton
Stockton, CA 95201
209 468-3345

Stockton City Shelter
1575 S Lincoln
Stockton, CA 95206
206 944-8274

Animal Welfare Groups

Humane Society of US
2100 L St.
Washington DC 20037
202 452-1100

Humane Society of US
West Coast Office
P O Box 417220
Sacramento, CA
916 344-1710

Am Soc Prevention of
Cruelty to Animals (ASPCA)
441 E 92nd. St.
New York, NY 10128
212 876-7700

American Humane Assn
63 Inverness Dr. E
Englewood, CO 80112
303 792-9900
800 227-4645

California Council of Companion
Animal Advocates
Priscilla Stockner DVM
619 745-4362

In Defense of Animals
415 453-9984

Animal Legal Defense Fund
415 459-0885

Fund For Animals
415 459-0885

Apartments for Pets

Peninsula Humane Society
415 340-8200

Artists, Dog

Petraits by Enid
Enid Zumar
415 883-9374

Behaviorists

San Francisco SPCA
415 340-8200 (Free Hotline)

Milly Robertson
415 591-9918

Gwen Bohnenkamp
415 647-8000

Angie Siegel
408 741-1936

Barbara DeGroodt
408 663-1675

Oz Training
408 629-7108

Julee Fullenwider
707 577-0560

Peninsula Humane Society
415 340-8200

Tom Mitchell
415 456-3232

Dr Ian Dunbar
510 658-8588

Kathleen Chin
800 675-0182

Marin Humane Society
415 883-0116

Debbie Mathis
408 TOP-PUPS

Karen Olson
510 825-0262

Bereavement Counseling

One of the drawbacks of dog ownership is the likelihood that we will outlive our beloved companions. Eight, ten, fifteen years down the line we are going to have to say goodbye.

Pet-Loss Counselors:

The Delta Society
PO Box 1080
Renton, WA 98057-1080
206 226-7357

SF SPCA
2500 16th St
San Francisco, CA 94103
415 554-3050

Pet Loss Support Hotline
School of Veterinary
Medicine, UC Davis
916 752-4200

Pet Loss Support Group
Jane Sorenson DVM
707 527-9330

Dog Owners Guide

Blood Banks for Dogs

These full service non-profit charitable blood banks ship canine blood products overnight to veterinarians anywhere in the United States that have a need. For more information call:

Hemopet Pet Life Line
Dr. W. Jean Dodds DVM
17672 Cowan #300
Irvine, CA 92714
714 252-8455
(Needs Dog blood donations)

San Diego Co Blood Bank
2317 Hotel Circle South
San Diego, CA 92108
619 299-7624

Boarding Kennels

The American Boarding Kennel Association
4575 Galley Rd. Ste. 400-A
Colorado Springs, CO 80915
719 591-1113

American Pet Boarding Association
312 634-9447

Books, Dog

Mail Order dog books:

4-M Enterprises, Inc
1280 Pacific St
Union City, CA 94587
800 487-9867 (Call for catalogue)

Dog Owner's
Home Veterinary Handbook
Delbert G. Carlson D.V.M.
James M. Giffin MD

The Complete Dog Book
by The Am Kennel Club

How to Teach A
New Dog Old Tricks
by Ian Dunbar

Playtraining Your Dog
by Patricia Burnham

Peak Performance
Coaching the Canine Athlete
M. Christine Zink DVM

Your Purebred Puppy
A Buyers Guide
by Michele Lowell

The Right Dog for You
by Daniel Tortora Ph. D

How to Be Your Dogs
Best Friend
Monks Of New Skete

Don't Shoot the Dog!
by Karen Pryor

How to Raise a Puppy
You Can Live With
by Rutherford & Neil

166

First Aid for Pets
by Robert W Kirk DVM
Sutton Books

*Atlas of Dog Breeds of
the World*
Chris & Bonnie Wilcox

Training Your Dog
J Volhard & G Fisher

*Active Years for Your
Aging Dog by Hershhorn*

*Your Dog, Its Development,
Behavior and Training*
by John Rogerson

*Coping With Sorrow
on the Loss of Your Pet*
by Moira Anderson

Cemeteries, Pet

My Pet Cemetery
430 Magnolia Ave
Petaluma, CA 94952
707 762-6743

Bubbling Wells
2462 Atlas Peaks
Napa, CA
707 255-3456

Whispering Pines
2601 Gravenstein Hwy S
Sebastopol, CA
707 823-5735

Chiropractic Care, Canine

American Veterinary Chiropractic Association

Dr. Sharon Willoughby
Port Byron, IL
309 523-3995

Salinas, CA
408 757-2009

Mark Lopes DC
Hayward, CA
510 537-1930

Michael Gleason DC
Hayward, CA
510 887-771-

Cinder Okuda DC
Santa Cruz, CA
408 423-3713

Michael Painter
Oakley, CA
510 625-1881

Kevin Haussler DVM
Davis, CA
916-756-9445

Stephanie Szabo
Sunnyvale, CA
408 720-1764

Gary Andreachi DC
Burlingame, CA
415 697-1446

K Ridgeway DVM
Garden Valley
916 333-2143

Complaints Against Veterinarians

The Board of Examiners in Veterinary Medicine regulates the
practice of veterinary medicine in California. Direct complaints to:

California Veterinary
Medical Association
5231 Madison Ave
Sacramento, CA 95841
916 344-4985

No Cal Vet Assoc
2505 Hill Top Dr
Redding, CA 96002
916 674-1600

Computer Bulletin Boards

Information bulletin boards on dog related subjects.

CompuServe $8.95 mo
Pet/Animal Forum
The Time Warner Dog
The Humane Society Forum
800 848-8199

GEnie $8.95 mo
Pet-Net
800 638-9636

America Online $9.95
Pets Forum under Lifestyles
800 827-6364

Prodigy $14.95 mo
Pets Bulletin Board
800 776-3449

Delphi $20 mo
Pet Lovers Forum
800 695-4005

DOGNET $70
Dog-only service
303 830-1113

Computer Software

Screen saver software.

Screen Magic Dogs
800 655-6244

Pet records system for all AKC required records, vaccinations, medical, all show records, pedigrees, stud contracts, sales receipts, entry forms and more. Call:

STARLINE
7131 Kermore
Stanton, CA 90680
714 826-5218

TiedWay Software
PO Box 662
El Segundo, CA 90245
310 631-8337

Den Trailing

Group of hunt instinct tests for breeds bred to hunt underground. Open to all terrier breeds and Dachshunds that can fit into a 9"square tunnel. Dogs stalk rats through tunnels ranging 10 to 30 feet. (This is a bloodless sport.)

Peter Kirkwood
707 823-2051

Doggie Day Care

Kamp K-9
Randy Ashton
707 795-5995

SF SPCA
415 554-3000

Education, Humane

Humane Education involves teaching children kindness and a caring attitude towards domestic pets and the humane treatment of all living creatures. Check with your local Humane Society.

Partners In Education
Training & Sharing (PETS)
Susan Daniels
RR # 6 Box 308 A
Tunkhannock, PA 18657
717 836-2753

Western Humane
Education Assoc.
Micki Zeldes
Marin Humane Society
171 Bel Marin Keys Bl.
Novata, CA 94947

Emergency Hospitals

If there is an after hour emergency call your Veterinarian. If he or she is unavailable then contact:

North Bay

Emergency Animal Hospital
4019 Sebastopol
Santa Rosa, CA
707 544-1647

Marin Veterinary Emergency
4240 Redwood Hwy
San Rafael, CA
415 472-2266

Solano Pet Emergency Clinic
4437 Central Pt
Cordelia, CA
707 864-1444

Animal Care Center of Sonoma Co
6620 Redwood Dr
Rohnert Park, CA
707 584-4343

Middletown Animal Hospital
21503 Hwy 29
Middletown, CA
707 987-2000

Silverado Veterinary Hospital
2035 Silverado Trail
Napa, CA
707 224-7953

East Bay

Alameda Co Emergency Pet Clinic
14790 Washington Ave
San Leandro, CA
510 352-6080

Tri Valley
6743 Dublin Blvd
Dublin, CA
510 828-0654

Pet Emergency Treatment Service
1048 University Ave
Berkeley, CA
510 548-6684

Animal Emergency Center
810 University Ave
Berkeley, CA
510 841-4412

Veterinary Centers of America
4820 Broadway
Oakland,CA
510 654-8375

Contra Costa Vet Emergency
1410 Monument Blvd
Concord, CA
510 798-2900

San Francisco Peninsula

All Animal Emergency Hospital
1333 9th Ave
San Francisco, CA
415 566-0531

St Frances Square Night Hospital
2179 Juniper Sierra Blvd
Daily City, CA
415 992-1100

No Peninsula Veterinary Emergency
217 N Amphlett Blvd
San Mateo, CA
415 348-2575

Park Animal Hospital
1207 Ninth Ave
San Francisco, CA
415 753-8485

Skycrest Weekend Veterinary Clinic
Skyline Blvd
San Bruno, Ca
415 588-1151

Pets Unlimited
2343 Fillmore
San Francisco, CA
415 563-6700

South Bay

S Peninsula Veterinary Emergency
3045 Middlefield Rd
Palo Alto, CA
415 494-1461

Emergency Animal Clinic San Jose
5440 Thornwood Dr
San Jose, CA
408 578-5622

United Emergency Animal Clinic
1657 S Bascom Ave
Campbell, CA
408 371-6252

Adobe Animal Hospital
396 1st St
Los Altos, CA
415 948-9661

Monterey Bay Area

Santa Cruz Veterinary Hospital
2585 Soquel Dr
Santa Cruz, CA
408 475-5400

Monterey Peninsula Emergency
2 Harris Ct
Monterey 408 373-7374 also
Salinas   408 663-6551

Animal Hospital at the Crossroads
3 Crossroads Mall
Carmel, CA
408 624-0131

Animal Hospital of Watsonville
150 Pennsylanis Dr
Watsonville, , CA
408 724-6391

Sacramento Area

Associated Veterinary Emergency
8311 Greenback Lane
Fair Oaks, CA
916 725-1711

Emergency & Intensive Care
9700 Business Park #404
Sacramento, CA
916 362-3146

Associated Veterinary Emergency
4990 Manzanita
Carmichael, CA
916 331-7430

Emergency Veterinary Care
6420 Freeport Blvd
Sacramento, CA
916 428-9202

Sacramento Emergency Veterinary
2201 El Camino Ave
Sacramento, CA
916 922-3425

El Macero Veterinary Clinic
417 Maci Blvd
Davis, CA
916 756-6764

Stockton Area

Associated Veterinary Emergency
3008 E Hammer Lane
Stockton, CA
209 952-8387

Tracy Area

Tracy Veterinary Clinic
20 W Grant Line Rd
Tracy, CA
209 835-0626

Fresno Area

Veterinary Emergency Service
1639 N Fresno St
Fresno, CA
209 486-0520

Modesto Area

Veterinary Emergency Clinic
1800 Prescott Rd
Modesto, CA
209 527-8844

Northern Counties

Veterinary Centers of America
2505 Hilltop Dr
Redding, CA
916 224-2200

Emergency Service Animal Med

Fortuna, CA
707 725-6131

Erickson Veterinary Hospital
11181 Midway
Chico, CA
916 343-5896

Cresent Animal Medical Center
1590 Northcrest Dr
Cresent City, CA
707 464-8321

Eye Care Registry

Canine Eye Registry Foundation

317 494-8179 (CERF)

Eye Care Specialists

Lewis Campbell
415 321-1218

Santa Rosa Animal Eye Center
707 571-8442

Field Trial & Hunting Test Clubs

American Kennel Club
Performance Events Div
51 Madison Ave
New York, NY 10010

National Hunting Retriever Club
PO Box 3179
Big Springs, TX 79721
915 267-1659

Dog Owners Guide

Monterey Bay Hunting Retriever
408 741-5946 Lucy

Redwood Empire Retriever Club
707 668-4161 Julie

Sagehen's Retriever Club
707 584-0154 Jane

Tamarin Spaniel Field Trial Club
2553 Michaelango Dr
Stockton, CA 95207
Dan Hale

Northern California Retriever Trial
707 664-1344 Ed

Sacramento Valley Retriever Club
707 864-1287 Barbara

San Jose Retriever Club
408 258-0418 Thomas

Flyball

Check with your local obedience or breed club.

North American Flyball Assoc
1 Gooch Park Dr
Barrie, Ont Canada L4M4S6
Glenn Hamilton

French Ring Sport

5325 W Hope Rd
Lansing, MI 48917
517 322-2221

Frisbee Competition

To be put on a mailing list and receive event info:

FriskiesCanine Frisbee
Disc Championship
4060-D Peachtree Rd. #326
Atlanta, GA 30319
800 786-9240
(Free training Booklet)

In California write/call:
Box 725
Encino, CA 91426
1 800 423-3268
818 780-4913

Greyhound Rescue

These groups work to save racing dogs that are scheduled to be killed.

Greyhound Pets of America
Darren Rigg
President & Founder
800 366-1472

Operation Greyhound
619 588-6611

Grooming, Dog

The National Dog Groomers Association of America
PO Box101
Clark, PA 16113
412 962-2711

Guide Dogs for the Blind

Guide Dogs of the Desert
P O Box 1692
Palm Springs, CA 92263
619 329-6257

Guide Dogs Of America
13445 Glenoaks Blvd.
Sylmar, CA 91342
818 362-5834

Guide Dogs for the Blind
PO Box 1200
San Rafael, CA 94915
415 479-4000

Handlers, Professional

Professional Handlers Association
Kathleen Bowser, Secretary (No Joke)
15810 Mount Everest Lane
Silver Springs, MD 20906
301 924-0089

Hearing Dog Programs

American Humane Assoc.
Hearing Dog Program
9725 E. Hampden Ave.
Denver, Co 80231
303 695-0811

San Francisco SPCA
415 554-3000

Canine Companions for Independance
707 528-0830

Dogs For The Deaf
10175 Wheeler Rd.
Central Point,OR 97502
503 826-9220

Paws with a Cause
1 800 253-PAWS

Herding

The Herdsman (AKC)
Rte 1, Box 52-A
Putman, Oklahoma 73659
405 661-2262

Debbie Pollard
916 687-8727

Cindy Billings
PO Box 8118
Woodland, CA 95695
SC Working Sheepdog Assoc

Marge Bankenship
707 643-6604

173

Dog Owners Guide

Kathy Christian
916 620-4159

Gail Oxford
209 727-3130

NC Working Sheepdog Assoc
916 485-2201

Joyce Shepherd
707 544-9562

Debbie Lehr (Old English Only)
916 687-7131

Holistic Veterinarians

This approach to health involves the consideration of everything that affects the patient's well-being, including lifestyle, environment, diet and exercise. This approach treats the causes as well as the symptoms of the ailment.

American Holistic Veterinary
Medical Association
2214 Old Emmorton Rd.
Bel Air, MD 21014
410 569-0795

Stephenie Chalmers
707 538-4643

Humane Societies

Berkeley Humane Society
2700 Ninth St
Berkeley, CA 94710
510 845-7735

Marin Humane Society
171 Bel Marin Keys
Novato, CA 94949
415 883-4621

Oakland SPCA
8323 Baldwin St
Oakland, CA 94621
510 569-0702

Santa Clara Humane Society
2530 Lafayette St
Santa Clara, CA 95050
408 727-3383

San Francisco SPCA
2500 Sixteenth St
San Francisco, CA 94103
415 554-3000

Contra Costa SPCA
1825 Salvio St
Concord, CA 94520
510 223-2271

Monterey County SPCA
1002 Monterey Salinas Hwy
Monterey, CA 93942
408 422-4721

Peninsula Humane Society
12 Airport Blvd
San Mateo, CA 94401
415 340-8200

Santa Cruz Anml Welfare & SPCA
2200 Seventh Ave
Santa Cruz, CA 95062
408 475-6454

Solano County SPCA
2200 Peabody Rd
Vacaville, CA 95696
707 448-7722

Humane Society of Sonoma Co
5345 Hwy 12 West
Santa Rosa, CA 95407
707 542-0992

Sacramento SPCA
6201 Florin Perkins Rd
Sacramento, CA 95828
916 383-7387

Palo Alto Humane Society
PO Box 60715
Palo Alto, CA 94306
408 327-0631

Ohlone Humane Society
PO Box 5118
Fremont, CA 94537
510 490-4587

Delta Humane Society
4590 S Hwy 99
Stockton, CA 95213
209 466-0339

Identification Suppliers

I D Tags

These companies will register your dog and issue special ID tags that allow them to put finders in touch with owners.

911-Pets Lost Service
1050 W 40th
Chicago, IL 60609
312 890-4911

Pet Find Inc.
P O Box 100
Gresham, OR 97030
800 243-2738

Petfinders
368 High St.
Athol, NY 12810
800 666-LOST

PeTag
800 PETAG-4U

TIP Use an O-ring rather than an S-hook to secure the tag to your pet's collar. There are a lot of dogs in the shelter with empty S-hooks hanging from their collars

ID-Microchip Services & Recovery

Microchip ID's are becoming increasingly common nationwide, but the method is only effective in an area where shelters are committed to using the scanner. Since there is more than one company marketing the method, a microchip might not be reliable if your shelter's scanner does not read the chip you purchased. Some animal organizations are waiting for standardization of scanners and chips before endorsing the method. An ID tag is still the best primary method, the pet is often returned before it gets to the shelter.

Avid Microchip
1 800 336-AVID

InfoPet Identification System
612 890-2080

Identichip ID & recovery system
717 275-3166

ID — Tattooing

Tattooing your dog for identification purposes won't do any good unless you register the tattoo with a national data bank.

National Dog Registry
Box 116
Woodstock, NY 12498
800 NDR-DOGS

Tattoo a Pet
1625 Emmons Ave.
Brooklyn, NY 11235
800 TATTOOS

U S Found
P O Box 521
Jarrettsville, MD 21084
410 557-7332

ID Pet
Box 2244 Dept D
Norton Hgts,CT 06820

Local Dog Tatoo Services

Renee Harris
415 552-1969

Patricia Stevens
408 226-3034

Rhonda
408 251-1720

Debbie Morton
408 377-2864

Debra Mitchell
916 737-2030

GG Couch
707 839-4253

Heather Hutchinson
510 825-0171

Kim Baskette
510 338-3374

Animal Health Care
209 436-4444

Insurance, Medical (for pets)

One reason for getting pet insurance is that it reduces the chances of having to put a dollar value on the life of your pet. Compare each policy in the areas of age of dog, cost per year, coverage limits, deductible, amount paid by policy and look for things NOT covered.

Veterinary Pet Insurance
800 345-6778

Appendix D: Service Directory

Licensing Info

All persons who own or shelter a dog over the age of 4 months must obtain a license. Your dog must have a current rabies vaccinations certificate before applying for the license. Licenses must be renewed each year. Contact your local shelter, humane society or police department to determine the place where you should apply.

South Bay Area

South Bay Animal Licensing
408 277-2965

West Valley Licensing
408 777-3180

Lobby Groups

Responsible Dog Owners Assoc.
242 Chapman Rd.
Doylestown, PA 18901
215 249-1370

Cal Fed of Dog Clubs
Vern Johnson
714 731-6428

Lure Coursing

American Sighthound
Field Assoc.
2108 Tranon Ct.
Tallahassee, FL 32308
904 877-6795

AKC Lure Coursing
Director
1235 Pine Grove Rd.
Hanover, PA 17331
717 637-3011 (Day)
717 632-6806 (Night)

Al Crume
27452 S Corral Hallow Rd
Tracy, CA 95376
209 836-5150

Kathy Kelly

John Fitzpatrick
510 793-9375

Magazines

Ask your national or local breed club for a recommendation on pure bred publications.

Dog Fancy
Subscription Dept
PO Box 53264
Boulder, CO 80323-3264

Front & Finish
The Dog Trainers News
P O Box 333
Galesburg, IL 61601

Gun Dog
P O Box 35098
Des Moines, IA 50315
515 243-2472

Hunting Retriever
United Kennel Club
Kalamazoo, MI 49001
212 696-8333

177

Dog Owners Guide

Hound Dog Magazine
P O Box 20
Holly Hill, FL 32117-0020
616 343-9020

Schutzhund Magazine
DVG America
PO Drawer P
Stanford, FL 32772

Off-Lead
P O Box 307
Graves Road
Westmoreland, NY 13490

Dog Watch
11331 Ventura Blvd. #301
Studio City, CA 91604

The Gazette
American Kennel Club
51 Madison Ave.
New York, NY 10010

Sighthound Review
PO Box 30430
Santa Barbara, CA
93130
805 966-7270

DogWorld
PO Box 6500
Chicago, IL 60680
800 247-8080

Memorials, Pet

Anderson Pet Memorials
207 Park Ave.
Carrollton, KY 41008
502 732-5860

Photo Pet Urns
909 627-3739

Pet Monuments
PO Box 995-A
Barre, VT 05641
802 454-1050

MLB International Urns
1 800 858-8767

Obedience Clubs

San Mateo Dog Training Club
4 Emerald Ct
San Mateo, CA 94403
Miriam Hillier
415 344-3240

The Del Valle Dog Club
510 455-4158 Carol Wilson

Marin County Dog Training Club
540 Marin Oaks
Novato, Ca 94949
415 461-6559

Davis Dog Training
PO Box 4878
Davis, CA 95613
Cherrie Brown
916 758-DOGS

Vallejo Dog Training Club
700 Sutter Creek
Vallejo, CA 95590
Christy Rose
707 448-6717

West Valley Dog Training
408 446-9208

County Wide Dog Training Club
1309 Tuliptree Rd
Santa Rosa, CA 95403
707 778-6689

Deep Peninsula Dog Training
3833 Park Blvd
Palo Alto, CA 94306
Laura Haar
415 424-8829

Dog Training Club of Salinas Vly
1445 Plumas
Seaside, CA 93955
Debbie Lafontaine
408 394-2731

Fresno Dog Training Club
8090 N Chamise Ln
Clovis, CA 93611
Gil Martinez
209 255-2960

Mt Diablo Dog Training Club
4435 Cottonwood Circle
Concord, CA 94521
Bonnie Heitz
510 933-8774

Oakland Dog Training
3524 Harbor View Ave
Oakland, CA 94619
Ellen Michael
510 482-3445

San Francisco Dog Training Club
PO Box 426202
San Francisco, CA 94142
Cindy Toste
415 585-2533

San Lorenzo Dog Training Club
1730 Grove Way
Castro Valley, CA 94546
Mary Tassey
510 483-4546

Golden State Kennel Club (UKC)
Jacki Root (Mixed Breed also)
916 967-5576

Town & Country Dog Training Club
408 226-6069

Fremont Dog Training
42277 Palm Ave
Fremont, CA 94539
Kimberly Silva
510 659-0324

Monterey Bay Dog Training Club
PO Box 287
Santa Cruz, CA 95061
Patti Burt
408 724-6657

Napa Valley Dog Training Club
3638 Jefferson St
Napa, CA 94558
Cheryl Hartman
707 253-8666

Sacramento Dog Training Club
5304 Illinois Ave
Fair Oaks, CA 95628
Gail Burnham
916 965-1253

San Joaquine Dog Training Club
13296 Alabama Rd
Galt, CA 95632
Sandy Schneider
209 477-2632

Santa Clara Dog Training Club
12366 Priscilla Lane
Los Altos Hills, CA 94024
Beverly Cobb
415 941-3221

Mixed Breed Dog Club of Cal
Chris Dane
415 588-1203

Humboldt Dog

Orthopedic

Orthopedic Foundation For Animals (OFA)
2300 Nifong Blvd
Columbia, MO 65201

Dog Owners Guide

Pedigree Service

Canine Pedigree Service
Rt 2, Box 168 Tally-Ho Rd.
Glyndon, MN 56547
218 498-2775

Pet Sitting

Look for a licensed, bonded and mature pet sitter who can provide references. Pets are generally happiest if they can stay at home, provided you can find someone responsible to take care of them. Professional services will come to your home and some will take care of your plants, mail, newspapers, as well as your pets.

Things They Should Know Before You Go
Where you can be reached in case of emergency
The name of your veterinarian

Payment arrangements in case of a medical emergency

Feeding, exercise and any medication instructions
What to do in case the pet becomes lost

National Association of
Professional Pet Sitters
1200 "G" St NW
Washington, DC 20005
800 296-PETS

Pet Photography

Take photos of your dog in a three quarter pose facing the camera. Dark breeds should have a light background and light or parti-colored pets need a solid dark background. Make sure it looks its best. It may be a good idea to place a picture in with your veterinary medical records. And you may need a picture for flyers if your dog is lost

Linda Kane   Margaret Coder
707 996-1060   415 924-4056

Cook PhoDOGraphy
408 688-7508

Poison Control

National Animal Control
Poison Center
University of Illinois
24 hour Hotline ($30)
1 800 548-2423
1 900 680-0000 ($20 min)

Poison Control Hotline
1 800 876-4766 SD
1 800 544-4404 LA

Registries, Dog

American Kennel Club
51 Madison Avenue
New York, NY 10010
212 696-8200 Main,
919 233-9767 Registration
212 696-8245 Library
212 696-8226 Gazette Subscription
919 233-9767 Customer Services

United Kennel Club.
100 E. Kilgore Rd.
Kalamazoo, MI 49001-
5592
616 343-9020

Canadian Kennel Club
100-89 Skyway Ave.
Etobicoke, ONT
Canada, M9W 6R4

Federation Canofila
Mexicana AC
Apartado Postal 22-535
14000 Mexico DF
905 655-1600

Rare Breeds
American Rare Breed Assoc
P O Box 76426
Washington, DC 20011
202 722-1232

Mixed Breed Dog Club of Cal
100 Acacia Ave
San Bruno, CA 94066
Chris Dane

Mixed Breeds
205 1st Street SW
New Prague,MN 56071
612 758-4598 or local
Kristen Hurley 714 523-8202

Rare Breed Dog Club of Am
PO Box 426260
San Francisco, CA
415 239-1181 eves

Research

This organization helps coordinate and provide funding for researchers throughout the nation who are attempting to improve veterinary care for pets and wild animals.

Morris Animal Foundation
45 Inverness Dr.
Englewood, CO 80112-5480
303 790-2345

Rescue/ Adoption Referral Organizations

Bay Area Canine Rescue (BACR)
415 325-3947

Conta Costa Animal Rescue Effort
510 685-1273

Companion Animal Rescue Effort
408 659-3238

Small Animal Rescue
510 524-7657

Hayward Friends of Animals
510 886-7546

East Bay Animal Referral
510 841-7297

Tri Valley Animal Rescue
510 484-0949

TLC Canine Rescue
415 364-6288

Nike Animal Rescue Foundation
408 224-NARF

Pets In Need
415 367-1405 Bay Area
916 451-1346

St Francis Rescue Society
408 778-1095

Pet Friends & Rescue
408 637-6898

National Rescue Groups

Project Breed
202 244-0065

Operation Greyhound
619 588-6611

Greyhound Pets of America
Darren Rigg
President & Founder
800 366-1472

Baja, Mexico

Friends of Bajas Animals
Ellen Tousley
619 291-9223

Service Dogs

These are dogs that are trained to help the disabled. Support Teams for Independence and Canine Companions for Independence are local organizations that are always looking for puppy raisers. All these organizations rely on financial contributions. Call to see how you can help:

Canine Companions for
Independence
P O Box 446
Santa Rosa, CA 95401
707 528-0830
Rancho Santa Fe Site
619 756-1012

Paws with a Cause
1-800-253-PAWS

Support Teams for Independence
Perris, CA 92572
909 943-3972

Schutzhund

United Schutzhund
Club of America
3704 Lemoy Ferry Rd.
St. Louis, MO 63125
314 638-9686

Landersverband DVG
America Inc.
Sandi Nethercutt
113 Vickie Dr
Del City, OK 73115
405 672-3947

Betty Evans
415 897-7311

SF Schutzhund Club
Pat Cooper
707 838-4538

Stanislaus Co Schutzhund Club
Peggy Park
209 869-3647

Contra Costa Schutzhund Club
Mike Shannon
510 531-0657

Coyote Valley Schutzhund Club
Joy Cliver
408 923-8085

Feather River Schutzhund Club
Shelly Reeker
916 671-7196

Menlo Park Schutzhund Club
David Witmer
415 364-6987

Monterey Bay Schutzhund Club
Julie Ortner
408 726-2670

Redwood Hundesport
Joyce Bruce
707 263-8359

Sacramento Working Dog Club
Mike Henderson
916 362-5652

Sledding Clubs

Glenda Walling
7118 N Beehive Rd.
Pocatello, ID 83201
208 234-1608

Donna Hawley
P O Box 446
Norman, ID 83848-0446
208 443-3153

Sherry Galka
209 532-9217

Spay/ Neuter (Low Cost) Directory

In 1991 California housed 493,000 dogs in 217 shelters. Of these:

296,000 or 60% were killed,
94,000 dogs or 19% were claimed by owner
103,000 or 21% of the dogs were adopted.
Please, spay or neuter your pet at an early age.

Spay Nueter Clinic Hotline
800 434-SPAY

Animal Birth Control Clinic
408 778-1095

Dog Owners Guide

Animal Protection Institute
PO Box 22505
Sacramento, CA 95822
916 731-5521

Planned Pet-Hood of Sonoma Co
Julie Hunter
707 524-3550

St Francis
408 778-1095

Peninsula Humane Society
415 340-8200

Marin Human Society
707 883-3383

Humane Society of the US
2100 L St NW
Washington, 20037
202 452-1100

SF SPCA
415 554-3000

San Jose Spay Nueter Clinic
408 436-1740

Palo Alto Animal Service
408 327-0631

Animal Birth Control Clinic
415 456-7515

Search & Rescue

Canine Search & Rescue (SAR) units are involved in using dogs to find lost people in various situations including wilderness, disaster, water, avalanche and urban situations. The different types of training are air-scenting, tracking/ trailing and water rescue work. National units such as the U. S. Disaster Dog Team are on ready status awaiting calls by local fire, police and emergency personnel.

Nat Assoc Search & Rescue
PO Box 3709
Fairfax, VA 22308

California Rescue Dog Assoc.
Shirley Hammond
1062 Metro Circle
Palo Alto, CA 94303
415 856-9669

SAR Dog Alert
PO Box 39
Somerset, CA 95684

Sporting Equipment

For items like Jumps, Tunnels, Dog Walks, A Frames, Teeter Totters etc.

Action K-9 Sports Equipment Co.
707 F East 4th St.
Perris, CA 92570
714 657-0227

184

Superintendents of Dog Shows

William Antypas
PO Box 7131
Pasadena, CA 91109
818 440-9439

Margery Brown
2242 London Ave
Redding, CA 96001
916 243-0775

Ace Mathews
PO Box 06150
Portland, OR 97206
503 233-4241

Jack Bradshaw
PO Box 7303
Los Angeles, CA 90022
213 727-0136

Thomas Crowe
PO Box 22107
Greensboro,NC 27420
919 379-9352

Jack Onofrio
PO Box 25764
Oklahoma, OK 73125
405 427-8181

Note: Entries close 3 weeks in advance of the event.

Temperament Testing

American Temperament Test Society
314 225-5346

Therapy Dogs

The following is a list of organizations that take pets to visit the elderly in day care centers and nursing homes. These groups believe that the well-being of the elderly and the disabled is enhanced by the company of pets.

The Delta Society, through its pet partners program, offers accreditation to volunteers and their pets in a national network of animal visitation programs.

Delta Society
P O Box 1080
Renton, Washington 98057
206 226-7357

Therapy Dogs Inc.
Ann Butrick
2416 East Fox Farm Rd.
Cheyenne, WY 82007
307 638-3223

Pet Assisted Therepy Service
408 280-6171

Hayward Friends of Animals
510 886-7546

Therapy Dogs Int'l
91 Wiman Ave.
Staten Island,NY 10308
718 317-5804

Therapy Dog International
260 Fox Chase Rd
Chester, NJ 07930

Ohlone Humane Society
510 490-4587

Friendship Foundation
510 528-9104

Dog Owners Guide

SF SPCA
415 554-3000

Pets Life Line
707 996-4577

Lend-A-Heart
Dianne Sipe
916 689-4530

Lita Pet Connection
415 472-5482

Hug A Pet
408 727-3383 x833

Check with your local Humane Society or Animal Control agency
for other local organizations.

Tracking Tests

American Kennel Club
51 Madison Ave.
New York, NY 10010
212 696-8286

Mildred Rothrock

United Kennel Club
100 E Kilgore Rd.
Kalamazoo, MI 49001-5592
616 343-9020

Palo Alto Foothills Tracking Assoc
Rita Carr
408 247-8196

Trainers Organizations

North America Dog
Obedience Instructors (NADOI)
Lonnie Morgan, President
810 655-4129

Association of Pet Dog Trainers
2140 Shattuck Ave. #2406
Berkeley, CA 94704
510 658-8588

Trainers

Julie Cairns
707 668-4161

Karen Clanin
805 466-3775

Linda Hause
707 544-6146

John & Linda Radcliff
916 988-2164

Lori Drouin
510 233-8422

Garnet Bowa
707 823-0379

Alan Miller
916 483-4452

Flo Bell
707 525-9575

Loretta Delinger
510 254-8353

Judie Howard
510 376-2074

Pam Hartley
408 982-0228

Barbara DeGroodt
408 663-1675

Joan Gertin (Common Sense)
916 485-2201

186

Travel Guides

Hotel & Motel Guides

Send for:
Touring with Towser ($3)
Quaker Professional Services
585 Hawthorne Court
Galesburg, IL 61401

California Dog Lovers Companion
by Maria Goodavage $16.95
Foghorn Press

Vacationing W/ Your Pet
Pet-Friendly Pub ($14.95)
1 800 496-2665

Transportation Services

Pet Express
1000 Iowa St
San Francisco, CA
415 821-7111

TLC Express
1831 Robin Hood Lane
Santa Rosa, CA
707 578-0436

Travel Regulations for Pets

Prepared by ASPCA Send $4 to:

"Traveling with your Pet"
The American Society for the
Prevention of Cruelty to Animals
Education Dept.
441 East 92nd St.
New York, NY 10128

Travel Safety for Dogs

Do-It
Bud Brownhill
2147 Avon Circle
Anaheim, CA 92804
714 776-9970

Veterinary Assoc.& Referrals

American Animal
Hospital Assoc
P O Box 150899
Denver, CO 80215-0899
800 252-2242

American Veterinary
Medical Assoc
930 N Meacham Rd.
Schaumburg, IL 60196
1 800 248-2862

California Veterinary Medical Assoc
5231 Madison Ave
Sacramento, CA 95841
916 344-4985

No Cal Vet Assoc
2505 Hill Top Dr
Redding, CA 96002
916 674-1600

Santa Clara Veterinary Med Assoc
Peninsula Veterinary Medical Assoc
408 356-8924

Video Tapes

Sirius Puppy Training
Dr. Ian Dunbar
Center for Applied Animal Behavior
2140 Shattuck Ave. #2406
Berkeley, CA 94704
510 658-8588

4 M Enterprises
510 489-8722
(Call for catalogue)

Volunteers

Contact your local humane society or animal shelter. These non-profit organizations provide foster care and homes for pets; donate resources and supplies to help shelters; run ads in local newspapers for found pets; assist the needy with impound fees and medical fees. Also, they assist at the shelters with fostering, animal care, pet-assisted therapy, mobile pet adoptions, humane education and fundraising projects. Some also have a thrift shop or antique shop that needs staffing.

Index

ORDER & REORDER FORM

TO: **CANINE LEARNING CENTERS**
P.O. Box 2010
Carlsbad, California 92018
619 931-1820

Enclosed is a check for $_____ for _____ copy(ies) of either of our current Dog Owners Guides:
Northern California Dog Owners Guide
Southern California Dog Owners Guide
As shown below, the price for each Dog Owners Guide is $9.95 each in quantities from 1-7 copies or $5.75 each book with a minimum order of 8 copies.

Coming Soon! Please watch for more regional Dog Owners Guides.

_____ Copies @ $9.95 each (1-7 copies) $_____

_____ Copies @ $5.75 each (minimum 8) $_____

California residents please add 7.75% Sales Tax $_____

Shipping charge ($3.50 for 1-10 books; $5.00 for 11+) $_____

TOTAL $_____

Ship to: _____

Address: _____

City/State/Zip: _____

Telephone: _____

SPECIAL OFFER FOR BREEDERS:

Help educate new puppy owners by offering a free book with each adoption. You save 40% and will provide your new owner with a Free Puppy Exam.

NEW & REVISED LISTINGS & SUGGESTIONS

We would like to receive your feedback on how to improve this publication. Anyone wishing to comment is invited to use this form to submit information or to request changes. Also, use this form if any other corrections are necessary. Please fill out the following and mail to:

CANINE LEARNING CENTERS
P.O. Box 2010
Carlsbad, California 92018

Name(s): _____

Old Address: _____

City/State/Zip: _____

Kennel Name: _____

New Address: _____

City/State/Zip: _____

New Telephone Number: _____

Other Comments or Suggestions: _____

_____

_____

_____

_____

_____

_____

IMPORTANT INFORMATION (Continued)

DATES:	TREATMENT / VACCINATION TYPE:

IMPORTANT INFORMATION

DOG'S NAME: _____ Date of Birth: ___/___/___

Breed: _____ Sex: _____ Kennel: _____

Breeder's Name: _____ Phone: _____

Sire: _____ DAM: _____

Veterinary Hospital: _____

Veterinarian's Name: _____

Phone #: _____ Emergency Phone: _____

Address: _____

_____ Zip: _____

Insurance Policy No.: _____ Insurance Phone: _____

DATES:	TREATMENT / VACCINATION TYPE:

Continued